VIRTUAL WHOLESALING
WEALTH

Master the Art of Remote Deals, Maximize Profits, and Transform Your Real Estate Business from Anywhere in the World

By

Daniel L. Lucero

Table of Contents

Introduction

Welcome to the world of Virtual Wholesaling Wealth, where the boundaries of traditional real estate investing are transcended, and the key to success lies in the realm of virtual transactions. In this dynamic era, where technology connects us across distances and transforms industries, the real estate market is no exception. The convergence of innovation and opportunity has given rise to a revolutionary approach in the real estate investment landscape — virtual wholesaling.

This book is your guide to unveiling the secrets of remote real estate success, providing you with insights, strategies, and a roadmap to thriving in the competitive world of virtual wholesaling. Whether you're a seasoned investor looking to adapt to the changing times or a newcomer eager to leverage the power of technology, the principles and tactics within these pages will empower you to navigate the virtual landscape with confidence.

In the following chapters, we'll explore the core concepts of virtual wholesaling, dissecting the intricacies of conducting deals from the comfort of your home or anywhere in the world. From leveraging online tools to building a virtual team, we'll delve into the practical aspects that make virtual wholesaling not just a possibility but a lucrative and scalable venture.

Prepare to discover how to identify lucrative opportunities, negotiate deals effectively, and close transactions seamlessly, all without leaving your computer screen. The secrets shared here are not just theoretical; they are tried-and-true methods employed by successful virtual wholesalers who have transformed the way they do business.

Whether you're seeking financial freedom, looking to diversify your real estate portfolio, or simply intrigued by the prospect of virtual wholesaling, this book is your gateway to a new frontier in real estate investing. Join us on this journey, and let's unlock the potential of virtual wholesaling together. Your success in the world of remote real estate awaits!

CHAPTER 1

UNDERSTANDING VIRTUAL WHOLESALING

Defining Virtual Wholesaling

In the dynamic landscape of real estate investment, the term "virtual wholesaling" has emerged as a transformative approach, redefining the way transactions are conducted and opportunities are seized. In this section, we will delve into the core definition of virtual wholesaling, unraveling its fundamental principles and outlining how it represents a paradigm shift in the real estate industry.

What is Virtual Wholesaling?

At its essence, virtual wholesaling is a real estate investment strategy characterized by the remote execution of property transactions. Unlike traditional wholesaling, which often involves physical presence and localized dealings, virtual wholesaling harnesses the power of technology and digital tools to facilitate transactions from a distance. This method enables investors to identify, secure, and sell properties without the necessity of being physically present in the target market.

Key Components of Virtual Wholesaling

1. **Digital Transactions:** Virtual wholesaling emphasizes the use of online platforms and digital tools to streamline the entire transaction process. From property identification and due diligence to negotiations and closing, each stage can be conducted remotely.

2. Remote Communication:

Effective communication is vital in any real estate transaction. Virtual wholesaling relies on virtual communication channels, such as video calls, emails, and messaging platforms, to maintain clear and efficient interactions between investors, buyers, and sellers.

3. Data-Driven Decision Making: Utilizing data analytics and market research, virtual wholesalers make informed decisions about potential deals. This reliance on data allows for a more strategic approach to identifying lucrative opportunities.

4. Global Reach: Virtual wholesaling breaks down geographical barriers. Investors can engage in transactions across different markets and even internationally, broadening the scope of potential deals and maximizing opportunities.

How Virtual Wholesaling Differs from Traditional Wholesaling

While traditional wholesaling often involves hands-on activities like property visits, local networking, and face-to-face negotiations, virtual wholesaling transcends these limitations. It's a departure from the conventional model, emphasizing a digital-first approach that enhances efficiency, scalability, and the ability to navigate a global marketplace.

The Evolution of Real Estate Investing

Virtual wholesaling represents a significant evolution in the real estate investing landscape. It leverages the capabilities of the digital age to create new possibilities for investors, opening doors to a more flexible, scalable, and technologically-driven approach to building wealth through real estate.

As we explore the nuances of defining virtual wholesaling, envision a future where geographic constraints no longer dictate the scope of your real estate endeavors. Welcome to a realm where innovation and opportunity converge to redefine the very essence of real estate investing.

The Advantages of Virtual Wholesaling

Virtual wholesaling brings forth a myriad of advantages for real estate investors. From eliminating geographic constraints to increasing operational efficiency, the benefits are transformative. The chapter will delve into how virtual wholesaling enables investors to scale their operations, reduce costs, and access a global marketplace, opening doors to opportunities that transcend traditional boundaries.

The Role of Technology

At the heart of virtual wholesaling lies technology. This section will explore the various tools and platforms that empower virtual wholesalers, from online marketplaces and data analytics to virtual communication and collaboration tools. Understanding the technological landscape is key to successfully implementing a virtual wholesaling strategy.

Building a Virtual Wholesaling Mindset

Beyond the mechanics, virtual wholesaling requires a mindset shift. Investors need to adapt to the idea that success can be achieved without a physical presence in the market. This chapter will delve into the mindset and skills necessary for thriving in the virtual realm, emphasizing the importance of adaptability, agility, and a keen understanding of digital tools.

As we embark on the journey of "Understanding Virtual Wholesaling," envision a paradigm where borders are no longer barriers, and the traditional constraints of real estate are redefined. Welcome to a world where innovation meets opportunity, and success is not bound by geographical limitations.

The Evolution of Real Estate in the Virtual Age

In the not-so-distant past, the world of real estate was deeply rooted in physical presence-handshakes, property visits, and face-to-face negotiations. However, as the digital age has unfolded, a profound evolution has occurred, reshaping the very fabric of the real estate industry.

In the early days of real estate, success often hinged on local networks, on-the-ground knowledge, and a physical presence in the neighborhoods where deals unfolded.

Fast forward to the present day, and the landscape looks vastly different. Technological advancements have birthed a new era, one where geographic boundaries are blurred, and transactions are executed in the digital realm.

This chapter explores the catalysts driving the evolution of real estate into the virtual age. We'll delve into the impact of technology on property discovery, deal sourcing, and transaction processes. From online marketplaces to data analytics, the tools available in the virtual age are revolutionizing the way investors approach the market.

Moreover, this shift has not only changed the logistical aspects of real estate but also redefined the very essence of what it means to be a real estate professional. The ability to conduct business virtually has opened doors to a global marketplace, allowing investors to explore opportunities far beyond their local confines.

As we navigate through, we'll uncover the challenges and opportunities presented by the virtual age. From the democratization of information to the rise of virtual teams, the transformation is profound. The journey into virtual wholesaling is not just a response to a changing landscape; it is an embrace of a new era where innovation and adaptability are the keys to success.

Differentiating Virtual Wholesaling from Traditional Methods

In the ever-evolving landscape of real estate investing, the distinction between virtual wholesaling and traditional methods is crucial for investors seeking innovative approaches to maximize their opportunities. This section explores the key differentiators that set virtual wholesaling apart from traditional methods, shedding light on how this evolution in strategy offers a paradigm shift in the industry.

1. Geographic Independence

- *Traditional Wholesaling:* In traditional wholesaling, the emphasis often lies on a physical presence in a specific market. Investors build relationships, attend local events, and conduct business within a defined geographic area.

- *Virtual Wholesaling:* Contrastingly, virtual wholesaling transcends geographical constraints. Investors can identify, negotiate, and close deals in markets far beyond their physical location, leveraging the power of online platforms and digital tools.

2. Transaction Efficiency

- *Traditional Wholesaling:* Traditional methods may involve time-consuming processes, such as physical property visits, in-person negotiations, and manual paperwork.

These aspects can contribute to a slower transaction timeline.

- *Virtual Wholesaling:* Virtual wholesaling streamlines processes through digital transactions, remote communication, and data-driven decision-making. The result is a more efficient and agile transaction timeline, reducing the time and effort required to close deals.

3. Technology Integration

- *Traditional Wholesaling:* While technology plays a role in traditional wholesaling, the reliance on in-person interactions and physical networking often takes precedence.

- *Virtual Wholesaling:* Virtual wholesaling places a strong emphasis on technology. Investors leverage online platforms for property discovery, data analytics for informed decision-making, and virtual communication tools for negotiations, creating a digital-first approach to real estate transactions.

4. Scaling Opportunities

- *Traditional Wholesaling:* Scaling traditional wholesaling operations can be challenging due to the need for a physical presence, localized teams, and on-the-ground infrastructure.

- *Virtual Wholesaling:* The virtual model allows for scalability without the same limitations. Investors can expand their reach and conduct business in multiple markets without the constraints of physical infrastructure, opening avenues for significant growth.

5. Global Reach

- *Traditional Wholesaling:* Traditional methods are often confined to a local or regional scope, limiting the reach and diversity of investment opportunities.

- *Virtual Wholesaling:* Virtual wholesaling provides a global reach, enabling investors to explore and engage in transactions across different markets and even internationally. This global perspective broadens the potential for lucrative deals.

Understanding these differentiators is pivotal for investors looking to navigate the evolving landscape of real estate. As we explore the contrast between virtual and traditional wholesaling, envision a future where flexibility, efficiency, and global connectivity redefine the very essence of real estate investing.

Why Virtual Wholesaling Works

The effectiveness of virtual wholesaling in the real estate industry can be attributed to several key factors that leverage technology, efficiency, and a strategic approach to transactions. Understanding why virtual wholesaling works involves recognizing the advantages it offers over traditional methods and how it taps into the evolving dynamics of the modern real estate landscape.

1. Geographic Freedom:

- *Traditional Wholesaling Limitation:* Traditional methods often tie investors to a specific geographic area, limiting the scope of potential deals.

- *Virtual Wholesaling Advantage:* Virtual wholesaling breaks free from geographical constraints, allowing investors to explore and capitalize on opportunities in markets far beyond their physical location.

2. Efficient Use of Technology:

- *Traditional Wholesaling Approach:* Traditional methods may involve manual processes, paperwork, and in-person negotiations, leading to slower transaction timelines.

- *Virtual Wholesaling Efficiency:* Leveraging digital tools, online platforms, and virtual communication, virtual wholesaling streamlines processes, significantly reducing the time and effort required to close deals.

3. Global Market Access:

- *Traditional Wholesaling Limitation:* Traditional approaches are often confined to local or regional markets, limiting the diversity of investment opportunities.

- *Virtual Wholesaling Strength:* Virtual wholesaling provides a global reach, enabling investors to explore and engage in transactions across different markets and even internationally. This broadens the horizon for potential lucrative deals.

4. Scalability Without Physical Constraints:

- *Traditional Wholesaling Challenge:* Scaling traditional wholesaling operations may require establishing physical offices, localized teams, and infrastructure, presenting logistical challenges.

- *Virtual Wholesaling Scalability:* The virtual model allows for scalability without the need for extensive physical infrastructure. Investors can efficiently expand their reach and conduct business in multiple markets.

5. Data-Driven Decision Making:

- *Traditional Wholesaling Limited Insights:* Traditional approaches may rely on local knowledge and personal connections, potentially limiting the depth of market insights.

- *Virtual Wholesaling Informed Decisions:* Virtual wholesalers leverage data analytics, online marketplaces, and comprehensive research to make informed decisions, enhancing the strategic aspect of investment.

6. Operational Cost Savings:

- *Traditional Wholesaling Overhead:*
  Traditional methods may entail significant overhead costs, including travel expenses, maintaining physical offices, and local team management.

- *Virtual Wholesaling Cost Efficiency:*
  Virtual wholesaling significantly reduces operational costs, allowing investors to conduct business efficiently and cost-effectively.

7. Adaptability to Changing Conditions:

- *Traditional Wholesaling Rigidity:*
  Traditional methods may face challenges adapting to rapidly changing market conditions due to localized dependencies.

- *Virtual Wholesaling Agility:*
  Virtual wholesalers can adapt swiftly to market changes, leveraging technology and

remote operations to remain agile in response to evolving conditions.

In essence, the success of virtual wholesaling lies in its ability to embrace the advantages offered by the digital age, providing investors with a flexible, efficient, and scalable approach to real estate transactions that aligns with the demands of the contemporary market.

The Promise and Potential of Virtual Wholesaling

In the ever-evolving landscape of real estate, the promise and potential of virtual wholesaling stand as beacons of opportunity, ushering in a new era of flexibility, efficiency, and expansive growth. Let's dive into the unparalleled advantages and untapped potential that this innovative approach holds for aspiring and seasoned real estate investors alike.

1. Unshackling Geographic Constraints

Traditionally, real estate has been a game heavily influenced by location. The need for physical presence in a specific market has often limited investors to their local surroundings. Virtual wholesaling, however, shatters these geographic constraints. It empowers investors to explore, analyze, and engage in transactions anywhere in the world, all from the comfort of their virtual workspace.

2. Increased Efficiency Through Technology

Technology is the driving force behind the efficiency revolution in real estate, and virtual wholesaling is at the forefront of this transformation. The promise lies in the multitude of tools and platforms that streamline processes—from property identification and due diligence to negotiation and closing.

Embracing technology not only saves time but also enhances accuracy and precision in decision-making.

3. Scalability and Flexibility

One of the most alluring promises of virtual wholesaling is scalability. The ability to scale operations without the constraints of physical infrastructure or location-dependent teams opens up new dimensions of growth. Virtual wholesaling is inherently flexible, allowing investors to adapt to changing market conditions swiftly and capitalize on emerging opportunities.

4. Cost-Effective Operations

The traditional model of real estate transactions often involves substantial overhead costs, from travel expenses to maintaining a physical office. Virtual wholesaling significantly reduces these operational costs. With a well-designed virtual workspace, investors can conduct their business efficiently and cost-effectively, maximizing returns on each transaction.

5. Global Networking and Collaboration

Virtual wholesaling facilitates global networking and collaboration, connecting investors, buyers, and sellers across borders. This interconnectedness not only broadens the scope of potential deals but also fosters a collaborative environment where insights and expertise from various markets can be shared and leveraged.

As we explore "The Promise and Potential of Virtual Wholesaling," envision a future where the limitations of traditional real estate are replaced by a borderless, efficient, and scalable model. Virtual wholesaling is not just a methodology; it is a paradigm shift, offering a promise of success and a potential for growth that knows no bounds.

CHAPTER 2

SETTING UP YOUR VIRTUAL WORKSPACE

Creating an effective virtual workspace is foundational for success in virtual wholesaling. It involves assembling the right tools, configuring your digital environment, and establishing protocols for efficient and secure remote operations. This section will guide you through the essential steps of setting up your virtual workspace for optimal performance in the world of virtual wholesaling.

1. Tools and Platforms:

Identify and integrate the necessary digital tools, such as:

- Online Marketplaces: Platforms for property discovery and deal sourcing.

- Communication Tools: Video conferencing, messaging, and collaboration platforms.
- Document Management: Cloud-based storage for secure document sharing and organization.
- Project Management: Tools for task tracking, team collaboration, and project organization.

2. Secure Virtual Environment:

- Implement cybersecurity measures to protect sensitive information.
- Use secure and encrypted communication channels.
- Invest in a virtual private network (VPN) to ensure secure data transmission.

3. Digital Communication Protocols:

- Establish clear communication protocols for virtual meetings, negotiations, and team collaboration.

- Ensure all team members are familiar with virtual communication tools and best practices.

4. Remote Collaboration Strategies:

- Define workflows for remote collaboration, including document sharing, version control, and task delegation.
- Utilize project management tools to track progress, assign tasks, and monitor team activities.

5. Hardware and Software Setup:

- Ensure all team members have the necessary hardware (laptops, webcams, microphones) and software (communication tools, project management software) for seamless virtual collaboration.

6. Data Analytics and Research Tools:

- Integrate tools for market research, data analytics, and property evaluation to inform your investment decisions.

- Stay updated on the latest technologies and trends in real estate data analysis.

7. Training and Onboarding:

- Provide comprehensive training for team members on virtual tools and protocols.
- Create onboarding materials and resources for new team members to quickly adapt to the virtual environment.

8. Backup and Recovery Plans:

- Establish robust backup and recovery plans for critical data.
- Regularly back up important documents and ensure access in case of technical issues.

9. Virtual Team Building:

- Foster a sense of teamwork and collaboration through virtual team-building activities.
- Use online communication platforms to engage team members and maintain a positive team culture.

10. Continuous Improvement:

- Regularly evaluate the effectiveness of your virtual workspace.

- Seek feedback from team members and make adjustments to improve efficiency and address any challenges.

Setting up your virtual workspace is not a one-time task but an ongoing process of refinement and adaptation. By investing time and effort into creating a well-organized and secure virtual environment, you'll position yourself and your team for success in the virtual wholesaling landscape.

Essential Tools for Virtual Wholesaling

Successful virtual wholesaling relies on a suite of essential tools that streamline processes, enhance communication, and facilitate efficient decision-making. Here are key tools you should consider integrating into your virtual wholesaling toolkit:

1. Online Marketplaces:

- Zillow, Redfin, Realtor.com: Utilize these platforms for property discovery, market analysis, and identifying potential deals.

- PropStream, DealMachine: Explore tools specifically designed for real estate investors, providing advanced features for deal sourcing and property analysis.

2. Communication and Collaboration:

- Zoom, Microsoft Teams, Google Meet: Use video conferencing tools for virtual meetings, negotiations, and team collaboration.

- Slack, Microsoft Teams, Trello: Employ messaging and project management platforms to enhance communication and streamline collaboration.

3. Document Management:

- Google Drive, Dropbox, OneDrive: Leverage cloud-based storage for secure document sharing, collaboration, and organization.

- DocuSign: Implement electronic signature solutions to streamline the document signing process.

4. Data Analytics and Research:

- Reonomy, DataTree, RealQuest: Access data analytics tools for in-depth market research, property evaluation, and due diligence.

- Google Analytics: Utilize web analytics for insights into online market trends and user behavior.

5. Customer Relationship Management (CRM):

- Podio, Zoho CRM, Salesforce: Implement CRM tools to manage leads, track interactions, and streamline communication with buyers and sellers.

6. Virtual Private Network (VPN):

- ExpressVPN, NordVPN:
  Enhance cybersecurity by using a VPN to secure your internet connection and protect sensitive data.

7. Project Management:

- Asana, Monday.com, Jira: Employ project management tools to organize tasks, track progress, and ensure efficient workflows within your virtual team.

8. Data Visualization:

- Tableau, Google Data Studio: Visualize data to gain actionable insights and make informed decisions based on market trends and performance metrics.

9. Virtual Phone Systems:

- RingCentral, Grasshopper, Google Voice: Utilize virtual phone systems for professional communication, voicemail, and call forwarding.

10. Online Marketing Tools:

- Canva, Adobe Spark: Create visually appealing marketing materials for property listings and promotions.
- Mailchimp, Constant Contact: Implement email marketing tools for targeted outreach to potential buyers and sellers.

11. Financial Management:

- QuickBooks, Xero: Manage finances, track expenses, and maintain accurate records for your virtual wholesaling business.

12. Marketplace Analysis Tools:

- Costar, Mashvisor: Access tools that provide comprehensive data and analysis of real estate markets, helping you make informed investment decisions.

13. Electronic Payment Platforms:

- Square, PayPal, Stripe: Facilitate secure and efficient online transactions, especially useful for earnest money deposits and other financial transactions.

14. Social Media Management:

- Hootsuite, Buffer: Manage and schedule social media posts to promote listings, engage with the audience, and build an online presence.

15. Backup and Security:

- Backblaze, CrashPlan: Implement backup solutions to ensure the security and accessibility of critical data.

Selecting and integrating these tools into your virtual wholesaling operations will not only enhance your efficiency but also position your business to capitalize on the dynamic opportunities presented in the digital real estate landscape.

Creating a Productive and Secure Virtual Environment

Building a productive and secure virtual environment is crucial for the success of your virtual wholesaling operations. This involves combining the right tools, implementing robust security measures, and fostering a collaborative culture within your virtual team. Here's a guide to creating a productive and secure virtual environment for your real estate business:

1. Collaboration Platforms:

- Utilize platforms like Microsoft Teams, Slack, or Trello to facilitate seamless communication and collaboration among team members.

- Establish clear channels for different aspects of your business, from lead management to deal analysis.

2. Secure Communication Channels:

- Encourage the use of encrypted communication tools for sensitive discussions, such as contract negotiations and financial transactions.

- Implement secure email platforms and consider using end-to-end encryption for confidential information.

3. Virtual Private Network (VPN):

- Require the use of a VPN to secure internet connections and protect data transmitted over virtual networks.

- Educate your team on the importance of VPNs for remote work security.

4. Multi-Factor Authentication (MFA):

- Enable MFA for all critical business applications to add an extra layer of security to user accounts.

- Ensure that team members are familiar with and regularly use MFA to access sensitive systems.

5. Regular Security Training:

- Conduct regular security training sessions to educate your team about potential cyber threats and best practices for maintaining a secure virtual environment.

- Stay informed about the latest cybersecurity trends and share relevant updates with your team.

6. Cloud-Based Document Management:

- Choose secure, cloud-based document management platforms like Google Drive or Microsoft OneDrive to store and share documents.

- Implement access controls and permissions to restrict sensitive information.

7. Endpoint Security:

- Require all team members to have updated antivirus software and endpoint security solutions on their devices.

- Regularly perform security audits on devices to identify and address potential vulnerabilities.

8. Regular Backups:

- Establish a routine for regular backups of critical business data.

- Ensure that backup systems are tested periodically to guarantee data recovery in case of unexpected events.

9. Secure Video Conferencing:

- Choose secure video conferencing platforms with end-to-end encryption for virtual meetings.

- Implement meeting passwords and control access to ensure only authorized participants join.

10. Data Encryption:

- Enable encryption for sensitive data, both in transit and at rest.

- Utilize tools that automatically encrypt emails containing confidential information.

11. Secure Wi-Fi Networks:

- Encourage team members to use secure, password-protected Wi-Fi networks to prevent unauthorized access.

- Consider providing guidelines for securing home Wi-Fi networks.

12. Employee Device Policies:

- Develop and communicate policies regarding the use of personal devices for work.

- Implement measures to ensure that personal devices used for work are secure and comply with company policies.

13. Incident Response Plan:

- Establish an incident response plan outlining the steps to be taken in the event of a security incident.

- Conduct regular drills to ensure that your team is prepared to respond effectively to security incidents.

14. Regular Audits and Assessments:

- Conduct regular security audits and assessments of your virtual environment to identify and address potential vulnerabilities.

- Stay proactive in addressing security risks as technology and threats evolve.

15. Secure Access to Tools:

- Implement role-based access controls to ensure that team members have access only to the tools and information necessary for their roles.

- Regularly review and update access permissions based on team changes.

By implementing these measures, you'll create a virtual environment that not only promotes productivity but also safeguards your business and client information. Regularly reassess and update your security practices to stay ahead of emerging threats and maintain a secure virtual workspace.

Maximizing Efficiency with Technology

Maximizing efficiency with technology is a cornerstone of successful virtual wholesaling. Leveraging the right tools and systems can streamline processes, improve collaboration, and ultimately boost productivity.

Here's a guide to help you maximize efficiency through technology in your virtual wholesaling business:

1. Automation Tools:

- Utilize automation tools for repetitive tasks, such as email campaigns, lead follow-ups, and document generation.

- Examples include Zapier, Integromat, or tools with built-in automation features in CRM platforms.

2. Customer Relationship Management (CRM) System:

- Implement a CRM system to manage leads, track interactions, and streamline communication with buyers and sellers.

- Customize your CRM to fit the specific needs of your virtual wholesaling business.

3. Document Digitization:

- Digitize and centralize important documents using tools like Adobe Acrobat or CamScanner.

-Implement electronic document signing platforms like DocuSign for seamless and secure transactions.

4. Cloud-Based Project Management:

- Adopt cloud-based project management tools like Asana, Monday.com, or Trello to organize tasks, track progress, and enhance team collaboration.

- Ensure real-time access to project updates and task assignments.

5. Virtual Communication Tools:

- Leverage video conferencing tools such as Zoom, Microsoft Teams, or Google Meet for virtual meetings, negotiations, and team discussions.

- Utilize messaging platforms like Slack or Microsoft Teams for quick communication and collaboration.

6. Digital Marketing Platforms:

- Utilize digital marketing tools for property listings, promotions, and outreach to potential buyers.

- Platforms like Canva or Adobe Spark can help create visually appealing marketing materials.

7. Data Analytics and Market Research:

- Leverage data analytics tools and platforms for in-depth market research, property evaluation, and informed decision-making.

- Stay updated on the latest trends in real estate data analysis.

8. Online Marketplaces and Real Estate Platforms:

- Use online marketplaces and real estate platforms like Zillow, Redfin, or PropStream for property discovery, deal sourcing, and market analysis.

- Explore platforms specifically designed for real estate investors, such as DealMachine or Reonomy.

9. Virtual Tours and 3D Imaging:

- Implement virtual tour technologies to showcase properties online.

- Use 3D imaging tools to provide a comprehensive view of properties to potential buyers.

10. Financial Management Software:

- Adopt financial management software like QuickBooks, Xero, or FreshBooks to manage finances, track expenses, and maintain accurate records.

- Ensure seamless integration with other tools in your tech stack.

11. Task Automation in Email:

- Implement task automation features within email platforms for efficient follow-up and lead management.

- Utilize tools like Boomerang or FollowUpThen to automate email reminders.

12. Collaborative Document Editing:

- Use collaborative document editing tools like Google Workspace or Microsoft Office 365 for real-time collaboration on documents and spreadsheets.

- Ensure all team members have access to the latest versions of critical documents.

13. Mobile Apps for On-the-Go Management:

- Leverage mobile apps for on-the-go management and quick access to essential information.

- Ensure that key tools and platforms have user-friendly mobile applications.

14. AI and Predictive Analytics:

- Explore AI and predictive analytics tools to identify trends, assess property values, and predict market changes.

- Stay informed about emerging technologies in the real estate industry.

15. Training Platforms for Continuous Learning:

- Implement online training platforms to keep your team updated on the latest technologies, industry trends, and best practices.

- Encourage continuous learning to stay ahead in the competitive real estate market.

By strategically integrating these technologies into your virtual wholesaling business, you'll create a more efficient and streamlined operation, allowing you to focus on key aspects of your business while leveraging the power of technology to drive success. Regularly assess and update your tech stack to stay aligned with industry advancements.

CHAPTER 3

FINDING LUCRATIVE VIRTUAL DEALS

Finding lucrative virtual deals in real estate requires a strategic approach, leveraging digital tools, market insights, and effective networking. Here's a guide to help you identify and secure profitable virtual deals in the world of virtual wholesaling:

Online Marketplaces:

- Explore popular online real estate marketplaces like Zillow, Redfin, Realtor.com, and PropStream for property discovery.

- Set up custom alerts based on your investment criteria to receive notifications about potential deals.

Data Analytics for Market Research:

- Leverage data analytics tools to analyze market trends, property values, and investment potential.

- Platforms like Reonomy, DataTree, or RealQuest can provide in-depth insights into specific markets.

Network on Virtual Platforms:

- Engage in virtual real estate forums, social media groups, and online communities to connect with other investors, real estate professionals, and potential sellers.

- Platforms like BiggerPockets, LinkedIn, or real estate-focused Facebook groups can be valuable for networking.

Direct Marketing and Cold Calling:

- Implement targeted direct marketing campaigns using email, social media, or direct mail to reach potential sellers.

- Consider using virtual phone systems for efficient cold calling campaigns.

Investigate Distressed Properties:

- Identify distressed properties through online databases or local government records.

- Reach out to property owners facing financial challenges and explore potential opportunities for virtual wholesaling.

Virtual Property Tours and 3D Imaging:

- Utilize virtual tours and 3D imaging to explore properties remotely.

- Collaborate with sellers to provide virtual property tours to potential buyers.

Collaborate with Local Wholesalers:

- Build relationships with local wholesalers who can act as your eyes and ears on the ground.

- Partner with local wholesalers to expand your reach and gain insights into specific markets.

Attend Virtual Real Estate Events:

- Participate in virtual conferences, webinars, and industry events to stay updated on market trends and connect with potential sellers and buyers.

- Network with other investors and professionals in the virtual real estate space.

Automate Lead Generation:

- Implement automation tools for lead generation, follow-ups, and tracking.

- Use platforms like Zapier or Integromat to streamline your lead generation process.

SEO for Virtual Presence:

- Optimize your online presence and website for search engines.

- Implement SEO strategies to increase visibility and attract potential sellers looking to sell their properties virtually.

Explore Virtual Auctions:

- Participate in virtual property auctions to discover potential deals.

- Online auction platforms can provide opportunities to bid on and acquire properties remotely.

Build a Virtual Team:

- Assemble a virtual team with expertise in various aspects of real estate, including property evaluation, legal matters, and marketing.

- Leverage the collective strengths of your team to identify and assess virtual deals effectively.

Collaborate with Real Estate Agents:

- Partner with virtual real estate agents who can assist in identifying and evaluating properties.

- Real estate agents may have access to exclusive listings and valuable market insights.

Stay Informed About Market Trends:

- Regularly monitor market trends, economic indicators, and changes in local regulations.

- Stay informed about shifts in buyer preferences and emerging opportunities in the virtual real estate space.

Continuous Learning and Adaptation:

- Engage in continuous learning to stay abreast of new technologies, tools, and strategies in the virtual wholesaling landscape.

- Be adaptable and adjust your approach based on market dynamics and evolving industry trends.

By combining these strategies and staying proactive in your approach, you can position yourself to find lucrative virtual deals, capitalize on opportunities, and thrive in the dynamic world of virtual wholesaling.

Navigating Online MarketPlace

Navigating online real estate marketplaces is a crucial aspect of virtual wholesaling. These platforms offer a wealth of property information, potential deals, and networking opportunities. Here's a guide on how to effectively navigate online marketplaces for virtual wholesaling:

Choose the Right Platforms:

- Identify popular online real estate marketplaces such as Zillow, Redfin, Realtor.com, and PropStream.

- Consider specialized platforms that cater to real estate investors, like DealMachine, Reonomy, or Mashvisor.

Set Clear Investment Criteria:

- Define your investment criteria, including location, property type, budget, and potential profit margins.

- Use these criteria to filter and narrow down listings on online marketplaces.

Create Customized Alerts:

- Take advantage of alert features on online platforms to receive notifications when new properties that match your criteria are listed.

- Set up customized alerts to streamline your property discovery process.

Analyze Market Trends:

- Leverage market data and analytics tools provided by these platforms to understand local market trends.

- Analyze historical data, pricing trends, and property values to make informed investment decisions.

Utilize Advanced Search Filters:

- Make use of advanced search filters on online marketplaces to refine your property search.

- Filters may include property size, number of bedrooms/bathrooms, and specific features.

Explore Off-Market Properties:

- Investigate features on certain platforms that allow you to access off-market or pre-foreclosure properties.

- Networking with local agents and wholesalers can also provide insights into off-market opportunities.

Engage in Virtual Tours:

- Take advantage of virtual tour options if available on the platform.

- Virtual tours provide a comprehensive view of the property without the need for physical visits.

Understand Property History and Data:

- Review property histories, transaction data, and any available reports on the online platform.

- Understand the property's background, ownership changes, and any potential issues.

Connect with Local Agents:

- Engage with local real estate agents who may have exclusive access to certain listings.

- Establish relationships with agents who can provide valuable insights into the local market.

Networking with Sellers and Buyers:

- Leverage the marketplace's networking features to connect with potential sellers and buyers.

- Building relationships within the platform's community can lead to off-market opportunities.

Stay Informed About Market Regulations:

- Be aware of any local or regional regulations impacting real estate transactions.

- Stay informed about changes in zoning laws, property taxes, and other regulatory factors.

Use Multiple Platforms:

- Diversify your approach by using multiple online marketplaces to access a broader range of properties.

- Each platform may offer unique features and opportunities.

Evaluate Neighborhood Information:

- Assess neighborhood information provided on the platform, including crime rates, school ratings, and local amenities.

- Understand the neighborhood context before considering a property.

Review Financing Options:

- Explore financing options and mortgage calculators available on some platforms.

- Understand the financial feasibility of potential deals using the provided tools.

Engage in Discussions and Forums:

- Participate in discussions and forums within the marketplace's community.

- Exchange insights with other investors, gain knowledge and expand your network.

Effectively navigating online real estate marketplaces requires a combination of strategic filtering, data analysis, and active networking. By mastering these tools and features, you can uncover lucrative virtual wholesaling opportunities and stay ahead in the dynamic real estate market.

Utilizing Data And Analytics to Identify Opportunities

Utilizing data and analytics is a powerful strategy for identifying opportunities in the virtual wholesaling space. By leveraging technology and analyzing market trends, you can make informed decisions and uncover lucrative deals. Here's how to effectively use data and analytics in your virtual wholesaling business:

Market Research and Data Sources:

- **Explore Comprehensive Databases:** Utilize real estate databases such as Reonomy, DataTree, or RealQuest to access detailed property information, ownership records, and market trends.

- **Government Records:** Tap into local government records, assessors' offices, and public databases for additional data on properties, tax assessments, and ownership history.

Define Investment Criteria:

- **Location and Property Type:** Clearly define your investment criteria, including preferred locations, property types, budget range, and potential profit margins.

- **Market Conditions:** Consider the current market conditions, economic indicators, and local factors that may influence property values.

Data-Driven Property Evaluation:

- **Comparative Market Analysis (CMA):** Conduct a CMA using data analytics to assess the value of a property in comparison to similar properties in the area.

- **Appreciation Trends:** Analyze historical data to identify trends in property appreciation or depreciation in specific neighborhoods.

Identify Distressed Properties:

- **Foreclosure Data:** Use foreclosure data and pre-foreclosure information to identify distressed properties that may present potential opportunities.

- **Financial Stress Indicators:** Look for financial stress indicators in property records, such as tax liens or overdue payments.

Predictive Analytics:

- **Predictive Modeling:** Explore predictive analytics models to forecast future market trends and identify emerging opportunities.

- **AI-Based Tools:** Consider AI-based tools that analyze large datasets to predict potential shifts in property values or market demand.

Market Trends and Demographics:

- **Demographic Data:** Utilize demographic data to understand the characteristics of the local population, potential buyers, and renters.

- **Employment and Economic Trends:** Monitor employment rates, economic growth, and industry trends that may impact the real estate market.

Virtual Wholesaling Platforms:

- **PropTech Solutions:** Leverage technology platforms designed for real estate investors, such as DealMachine, to access data, analyze properties, and streamline deal sourcing.

- **Integrated Analytics:** Choose platforms that offer integrated analytics tools for comprehensive property evaluation.

Evaluate Rental Income Potential:

- **Rental Yield Calculations:** Analyze rental yield potential by considering property prices, rental rates, and vacancy rates in the area.

- **Local Rent Comparisons:** Compare rental rates in the target area to understand the demand for rental properties.

Assess Historic Sales Data:

- **Sale Price Trends:** Review historical sales data to identify patterns in sale prices and market fluctuations.

- **Seasonal Patterns:** Consider seasonal variations that may impact property sales and pricing.

Social Media and Online Presence:

- **Online Sentiment Analysis**: Monitor social media and online forums for sentiment analysis regarding specific neighborhoods or property types.

- **Online Presence of Sellers:** Evaluate the online presence of potential sellers to gauge their motivation and situation.

Networking and Collaborative Data:

- **Collaborate with Local Wholesalers:** Network with local wholesalers and investors to share insights and collaborate on data collection.

- **Crowdsourced Data Platforms:** Explore crowdsourced data platforms where investors share information about local markets and potential deals.

Environmental and Zoning Data:

- **Zoning Regulations:** Analyze zoning regulations to understand potential restrictions or opportunities for property development.

- **Environmental Impact:** Consider environmental data to identify properties with potential challenges or opportunities based on their surroundings.

Evaluate School Districts:

- **School Ratings:** Consider school district ratings and educational quality in the area, as this can influence property values and demand.

- **Neighborhood Stability:** Stable neighborhoods with good schools often attract long-term residents.

Scenario Analysis:

- **Sensitivity Analysis:** Conduct sensitivity analysis to assess how changes in various factors (interest rates, property taxes, etc.) may impact potential deals.

- **Risk Assessment:** Evaluate potential risks and uncertainties associated with each deal through scenario analysis.

Continuous Learning and Adaptation:

- **Stay Informed:** Regularly update your knowledge of data analytics tools, emerging technologies, and trends in the real estate market.

- **Adapt to Changes:** Be adaptable and adjust your strategies based on the evolving data landscape and market conditions.

By incorporating these data and analytics strategies into your virtual wholesaling business, you can gain a competitive edge, identify lucrative opportunities, and make informed decisions that lead to successful deals. Regularly reassess and refine your data-driven approach to stay ahead in the dynamic real estate market.

Uncovering Off-Market Gems

Uncovering off-market gems is a valuable skill in virtual wholesaling, as it allows you to access potential deals that may not be publicly listed. Here are some steps on how to effectively discover and pursue off-market opportunities:

Network with Local Wholesalers:

- Build relationships with local wholesalers who may have insights into off-market properties.

- Collaborate with experienced wholesalers to gain access to their network and potential off-market leads.

Connect with Real Estate Agents:

- Establish connections with real estate agents who might have pocket listings or exclusive off-market opportunities.

- Communicate your criteria and interests to agents who can keep you in mind for off-market deals.

Engage in Local Real Estate Meetings:

- Attend local real estate meetups, networking events, and investment clubs.

- These gatherings often provide opportunities to connect with property owners, investors, and industry professionals who may know of off-market properties.

Utilize Online Wholesaling Platforms:

- Explore online wholesaling platforms that specialize in off-market deals.

- Platforms like DealMachine or Realeflow may provide access to exclusive listings and off-market opportunities.

Direct Mail Campaigns:

- Implement targeted direct mail campaigns to property owners in your target area.

- Craft personalized and compelling messages to capture the attention of potential sellers who may be considering selling off-market.

Cold Calling and Outreach:

- Engage in cold-calling campaigns to property owners in your chosen neighborhoods.

- Develop a script and strategy for effective outreach to identify potential off-market opportunities.

Drive for Dollars:

- Physically drive or virtually explore neighborhoods to identify distressed or vacant properties.

- Use mobile apps like DealMachine to streamline the process of identifying and contacting property owners.

Connect on Social Media:

- Join local real estate groups on social media platforms.

- Engage with property owners and other investors who may share off-market opportunities within these groups.

Engage in Local Community Events:

- Attend community events and engage with locals.

- Word of mouth and personal connections can sometimes lead to off-market deals.

Establish a Strong Online Presence:

- Create a professional and informative website to showcase your expertise and interest in off-market deals.

- Encourage property owners to reach out to you directly.

Utilize Public Records and Data Platforms:

- Explore public records and data platforms to identify potential off-market opportunities.

- Look for indicators such as absentee owners, tax delinquencies, or properties with long ownership tenure.

Work with Distressed Property Owners:

- Identify distressed property owners who may be motivated to sell off-market.

- Reach out with solutions tailored to their specific situation.

Engage in Door Knocking:

- Door knocking is a direct and personal approach to identifying potential off-market deals.

- Be prepared with information about your services and the benefits of selling to you.

Collaborate with Property Managers:

- Establish relationships with property managers who may have insight into owners looking to sell off-market.

- Offer incentives for property managers who refer off-market opportunities to you.

Investigate Expired Listings:

- Research expired listings that have been taken off the market.

- Contact the property owners to explore whether they are still interested in selling and open to off-market deals.

Be Persistent and Consistent:

- Consistency is key in uncovering off-market gems.

- Stay persistent in your outreach and marketing efforts, as off-market opportunities may take time to surface.

Use Virtual Assistant Services:

- Employ virtual assistants to conduct research and outreach on potential off-market properties.

- Virtual assistants can help streamline the process of identifying leads.

Participate in Real Estate Auctions:

- Attend or participate in real estate auctions where off-market properties may be available.

- Network with other participants to explore potential deals.

Legal Notices and Probate Records:

- Monitor legal notices and probate records for potential off-market opportunities.

- These records may indicate properties that are not actively listed but are available for sale.

Offer Creative Solutions:

- Position yourself as a problem solver who can provide creative solutions for property owners.

- Tailor your approach based on the unique needs of each potential seller.

Remember, the key to success in uncovering off-market gems is a combination of networking, targeted marketing, and persistent outreach. By diversifying your strategies and consistently engaging with potential leads, you increase your chances of discovering lucrative off-market opportunities in the virtual wholesaling space.

CHAPTER 4

ASSEMBLING A REMOTE DREAM TEAM

Building a virtual team is essential for the success of your virtual wholesaling business. A well-organized and efficient team can streamline processes, enhance productivity, and contribute to the overall growth of your business. Here's a step-by-step guide on how to build a virtual team for your virtual wholesaling endeavors:

Define Roles and Responsibilities:

- Clearly define the roles and responsibilities needed for your virtual wholesaling team.

- Identify key functions such as lead generation, property analysis, negotiations, marketing, and administrative support.

Identify Necessary Skills:

- Identify the specific skills required for each role within your virtual team.

- Consider skills such as real estate expertise, digital marketing, data analysis, negotiation, and communication.

Recruitment and Hiring:

- Utilize online platforms and job boards to advertise virtual positions.

- Conduct thorough interviews to assess candidates' skills, experience, and compatibility with a virtual work environment.

Leverage Freelancers and Contractors:

- Consider hiring freelancers or contractors for specific tasks or projects.

- Platforms like Upwork, Fiverr, and Freelancer can connect you with professionals in various fields.

Establish Communication Protocols:

- Set clear communication protocols to ensure effective collaboration among virtual team members.

- Choose communication tools such as Slack, Microsoft Teams, or Zoom for regular meetings, updates, and discussions.

Provide Training and Onboarding:

- Develop comprehensive training materials and resources for new team members.

- Conduct virtual onboarding sessions to familiarize new hires with your business processes, tools, and expectations.

Implement Project Management Tools:

- Utilize project management tools like Asana, Trello, or Monday.com to organize tasks, track progress, and assign responsibilities.

- Ensure that team members have access to these tools for efficient collaboration.

Digital Collaboration Platforms:

- Implement digital collaboration platforms for real-time collaboration on documents and projects.

- Google Workspace or Microsoft Office 365 can facilitate seamless collaboration and file sharing.

Emphasize Accountability:

- Foster a culture of accountability within your virtual team.

- Clearly communicate expectations, deadlines, and performance metrics to ensure everyone understands their responsibilities.

Regular Team Meetings:

- Schedule regular virtual team meetings to discuss progress, address challenges, and foster a sense of teamwork.

- Use video conferencing tools for face-to-face interactions to strengthen team connections.

Encourage Open Communication:

- Encourage open communication and feedback within the team.

- Establish channels for team members to express ideas, share concerns, and contribute to decision-making processes.

Cultivate a Positive Virtual Culture:

- Foster a positive virtual culture by recognizing and appreciating team members' contributions.

- Implement virtual team-building activities to strengthen connections and morale.

Set Clear Goals and Objectives:

- Clearly communicate the overall goals and objectives of your virtual wholesaling business.

- Ensure that each team member understands how their role contributes to the larger vision.

Utilize Virtual Assistant Services:

- Consider leveraging virtual assistant services for specific tasks, such as research, data entry, or administrative support.

- Virtual assistants can enhance efficiency and productivity within your virtual team.

Invest in Professional Development:

- Support the professional development of your virtual team members.

- Provide access to training resources, webinars, and industry events to keep skills current and foster continuous improvement.

Regular Performance Reviews:

- Conduct regular performance reviews to assess individual and team performance.

- Use these reviews to identify strengths, address challenges, and set goals for improvement.

Flexible Work Arrangements:

- Be flexible with work arrangements to accommodate different time zones and individual preferences.

- Consider asynchronous communication for tasks that don't require real-time collaboration.

Employee Well-being:

- Prioritize the well-being of your virtual team members.

- Encourage a healthy work-life balance and provide resources for mental health and well-being.

Document Standard Operating Procedures (SOPs):

- Document standard operating procedures for key processes within your virtual wholesaling business.

- SOPs serve as valuable resources for training new team members and maintaining consistency.

Adapt and Iterate:

- Regularly assess the performance of your virtual team and the effectiveness of your virtual work processes.

- Be willing to adapt and iterate based on feedback and changing business needs.

Building a successful virtual team is an ongoing process that requires attention to detail, effective communication, and a commitment to fostering a positive and collaborative virtual work environment. By implementing these strategies, you can create a virtual team that contributes to the growth and success of your virtual wholesaling business.

Communication Strategies For Virtual Success

Effective communication is crucial for the success of virtual wholesaling, especially when your team is dispersed. Here are communication strategies to enhance collaboration and productivity in a virtual setting:

Choose the Right Communication Tools:

- Utilize a combination of communication tools such as Slack, Microsoft Teams, Zoom, and email.

- Tailor your tool selection to the type of communication (instant messaging, video calls, asynchronous updates).

Establish Clear Communication Channels:

- Clearly define the purpose of each communication channel.

- Use specific channels for project updates, general discussions, and team announcements.

Regular Team Meetings:

- Schedule regular team meetings to discuss ongoing projects, goals, and challenges.

- Use video conferencing for face-to-face interactions and to strengthen team connections.

Utilize Video Conferencing:

- Encourage the use of video during meetings to enhance visual communication.

- Video conferencing fosters a more personal connection among team members.

Define Communication Expectations:

- Clearly communicate expectations regarding response times.

- Establish guidelines for when and how team members should respond to messages.

Provide Detailed Project Updates:

- Encourage team members to provide detailed project updates regularly.

- Use project management tools to centralize information and track progress.

Document Communication Protocols:

- Document communication protocols and make them easily accessible to the team.

- Clearly outline the preferred modes of communication for different scenarios.

Encourage Open Communication:

- Foster a culture of open communication where team members feel comfortable sharing ideas and concerns.

- Create channels for feedback and suggestions.

Use Visual Aids:

- Utilize visual aids, such as charts and graphs, during virtual meetings.

- Visuals can help convey information more effectively, especially in a remote setting.

Establish Virtual Office Hours:

- Set virtual office hours for team members to be available for real-time communication.

- This creates designated times for team collaboration and discussions.

Clarify Expectations in Written Form:

- Clearly document expectations, guidelines, and project details in written form.

- Written communication helps prevent misunderstandings and serves as a reference.

Encourage Active Listening:

- Emphasize the importance of active listening during virtual meetings.

- Use techniques like summarizing and asking clarifying questions to ensure everyone is on the same page.

Utilize Project Management Tools:

- Leverage project management tools for task assignments, timelines, and collaboration.

- Tools like Asana or Trello keep everyone organized and informed about project statuses.

Celebrate Achievements and Milestones:

- Acknowledge and celebrate team achievements and milestones.

- Recognition boosts morale and fosters a positive team culture.

Implement Transparent Communication:

- Emphasize transparency in communication, especially for important updates or changes.

- Keep team members informed about the state of the business and any relevant developments.

Facilitate Casual Virtual Interactions:

- Create opportunities for casual interactions through virtual coffee breaks or social events.

- Casual conversations help build relationships and camaraderie among team members.

Establish Emergency Communication Protocols:

- Define emergency communication protocols for urgent situations.

- Ensure all team members are aware of the procedures for handling critical issues.

Training on Communication Tools:

- Provide training on the use of communication tools.

- Ensure that team members are proficient in the tools necessary for effective virtual collaboration.

Adapt Communication to Individual Preferences:

- Recognize and adapt communication styles to individual preferences.

- Some team members may prefer written communication, while others may prefer verbal communication.

Regularly Seek Feedback:

- Regularly seek feedback on the effectiveness of communication strategies.

- Make adjustments based on team input to continuously improve communication processes.

By implementing these communication strategies, you can foster a collaborative and efficient virtual work environment for your virtual wholesaling team. Clear and effective communication is essential for overcoming the challenges of remote work and achieving success in the virtual space.

Outsourcing and Delegating Effectively

Having the ability to successfully delegate tasks and outsource work are two abilities that are essential for improving your virtual wholesaling firm. The following is a guide that will assist you in maximizing the benefits of outsourcing and delegating to boost productivity and concentrate on the strategic parts of your company:

Determine Which Tasks Should Be Outsourced:

- Determine the duties that may be assigned or outsourced, and evaluate the amount of work that you have to do.

- Give more priority to activities that require specialized expertise, are time-consuming, or involve repeated tasks.

Having a Solid Understanding of Your Core Competencies:

- Find out what your primary talents are, and center your attention on the activities that play to your strengths.

- Delegate jobs that lie beyond your competence to professionals who can handle them more effectively.

Set Clear Objectives:

- Clearly state the goals of the work you wish to assign.

- Provide explicit instructions and expectations to guarantee clarity.

Choose the Right Outsourcing Partners:

- Research and pick trusted outsourcing partners or freelancers.

- Consider variables such as knowledge, reputation, and historical success.

Utilize Outsourcing Platforms:

- Leverage outsourcing services like Upwork, Fiverr, or Freelancer to discover experienced people.

- Use these networks to connect with freelancers that specialize in real estate-related jobs.

Build a Virtual Team:

- Assemble a virtual staff with unique abilities to handle different elements of your organization.

- Consider employing virtual assistants, researchers, marketers, and other professionals.

Effective Communication:

- Establish open communication routes with your outsourced crew.

- Use collaboration technologies like Slack or Microsoft Teams for real-time communication.

Set Realistic Deadlines:

- Set reasonable timelines for allocated activities.

- Consider time zone variances when creating deadlines for a multinational team.

Provide Adequate Training:

- Offer extensive training for outsourced team members.

- Ensure they have a comprehensive grasp of your company procedures and expectations.

Regular Check-ins and Updates:

- Schedule frequent check-ins and updates to monitor progress.

- Use video conferencing to promote face-to-face conversations for a more personal touch.

Implement Quality Control Measures:

- Implement quality control procedures to guarantee the accuracy and quality of work.

- Set benchmarks and examine the output often.

Protect Sensitive Information:

- Establish processes to secure sensitive information while outsourcing work.

- Use secure routes and technologies for file sharing and communication.

Delegate Non-Core Tasks:

- Delegate non-core jobs to free up your time for strategic pursuits.

- Focus on tasks that directly contribute to the development and profitability of your firm.

Monitor Key Performance Indicators (KPIs):

- Define important performance measures for assigned jobs.

- Regularly analyze KPIs to determine the efficacy of outsourcing agreements.

Adaptability and Flexibility:

- Be versatile and flexible in your approach to outsourcing.

- Adjust plans depending on the growing demands of your organization.

Document Standard Operating Procedures (SOPs):

- Document standard operating procedures (SOPs) for assigned responsibilities.
- SOPs serve as reference documents and guarantee uniformity in procedures.

Encourage Feedback and Collaboration:

- Foster a climate of cooperation and open communication.
- Encourage team members to share feedback on procedures and recommend changes.

Evaluate Cost vs. Value:

- Assess the cost-effectiveness of outsourcing tasks.
- Consider the value contributed to your company relative to the expenditures involved.

Build Redundancy:

- Avoid depending significantly on a single outsourced person or team.

- Build redundancy to reduce risks associated with unanticipated occurrences.

Continuous Improvement:

- Continuously analyze and enhance your outsourcing and delegating practices.

- Learn from experiences and change your technique to enhance efficiency.

By efficiently outsourcing and delegating work, you can simplify your operations, boost productivity, and concentrate on the strategic areas of your virtual wholesaling firm. Developing a well-coordinated team, whether in-house or virtual, helps you to use varied talents and knowledge for overall company success.

CHAPTER 5

MASTERING VIRTUAL NEGOTIATION TECHNIQUES IN REAL ESTATE WHOLESALING

In the domain of real estate wholesaling, the ability to bargain successfully is a game-changer, and mastering virtual negotiating skills has become critical for success. This chapter exposes a thorough approach to improving your talents, adjusting to the digital world, and assuring lucrative results in your virtual interactions.

A. Navigating the Virtual Terrain

Understanding the Virtual Dynamics

- Uncover the unique characteristics of bargaining in a virtual world.

- Adapt classic bargaining methods to prosper in the digital environment.

Building Trust Remotely

- Establish confidence with vendors and buyers via virtual channels.

- Leverage technology to build a trustworthy and transparent negotiating process.

B. Strategies for Virtual Negotiation Mastery

Effective Communication Techniques

- Fine-tune your communication abilities for virtual discussions.

- Utilize video conferencing, clear articulation, and active listening to boost your effectiveness.

Leveraging Data and Market Insights

- Harness the power of data and market insights during negotiations.

- Showcase your knowledge by bringing pertinent facts and trends into your conversations.

Negotiation Psychology in a Virtual Space

- Explore the psychological implications of virtual negotiating.

- Understand how human behavior impacts negotiating results and modify your strategy appropriately.

C. Overcoming Challenges in Virtual Negotiations

Addressing Cultural Differences

- Navigate cultural subtleties in virtual conversations.

- Develop an understanding of cultural sensitivities and change your communication approach appropriately.

Handling Objections and Concerns

- Anticipate and answer concerns virtually.

- Develop solutions to address frequent worries and objections voiced by sellers and purchasers.

D. Advanced Techniques for Virtual Wholesaling Negotiations

Creative Deal Structuring in the Virtual Space

- Explore new deal structuring approaches.

- Tailor your approach to generate win-win circumstances for all parties involved.

Utilizing Technology for Negotiation Advantage

- Harness technological tools for negotiating efficiency.

- Discover tools and applications that boost your capacity to negotiate and conclude agreements digitally.

E. Case Studies: Real-Life Virtual Negotiation Successes

Learning from Successful Virtual Deals

- Dive into real-life case studies of effective virtual discussions.

- Extract significant lessons and use them in your own virtual wholesaling agreements.

F. Preparing for Future Virtual Negotiation Trends

Adapting to Emerging Technologies

- Stay ahead by responding to developing technology in virtual negotiating.

- Explore the possible influence of AI, virtual reality, and other advances on the bargaining scene.

Continuous Learning and Improvement

- Embrace an attitude of constant learning in virtual negotiating.

- Commit to continual improvement, being updated about industry trends, and perfecting your bargaining skills.

Whether you're a seasoned negotiator or stepping into the virtual arena for the first time, the insights and methods given here will equip you to negotiate the complexity of virtual negotiations and obtain profitable transactions in the digital era.

Welcome to the future of real estate negotiation, where understanding the virtual environment is the key to unlocking extraordinary success.

Overcoming Challenges in Remote Deal-Making

In the ever-evolving environment of real estate, distant deal-making has grown more popular, driven by technical improvements and the rising desire for quick, flexible transactions. While the virtual sphere provides unparalleled prospects, it also poses new hurdles that professionals must adeptly manage to achieve success in distant deal-making.

Understanding the Remote Deal-Making Landscape

Remote deal-making includes the negotiation, execution, and conclusion of real estate deals without the necessity for physical presence.

This method offers for larger market reach, better efficiency, and the capacity to respond to the needs of a worldwide economic environment. However, the route towards effective remote deal-making is not without its hurdles.

Challenges in Remote Deal-Making

1. Communication Barriers:

- **Challenge:** The absence of face-to-face contact may lead to misunderstandings, misinterpretations, and a loss of personal connection.

- **Strategy:** Utilize video conferencing, clear textual communication, and collaborative technologies to overcome the communication gap. Establishing frequent check-ins and virtual meetings helps preserve a feeling of connection among deal participants.

2. Building and Maintaining Trust:

- **Challenge:** Establishing trust remotely may be tough when human interactions are restricted.

- **Strategy:** Prioritize transparency and openness. Provide complete information, employ virtual tours, and harness technology to establish a transparent deal-making process. Establishing a regular and trustworthy internet presence also adds to creating trust over time.

3. Overcoming Time Zone Differences:

- **Challenge:** Coordinating deal-related activity across several time zones might lead to delays and interruptions.

- **Strategy:** Implement flexible scheduling, utilize asynchronous communication mechanisms when practical, and set explicit expectations for response times. Leverage time zone management technologies to ease collaboration and guarantee timely communication.

4. Navigating Legal and Regulatory Variances:

- **Challenge**: Real estate transactions generally entail compliance with multiple legal and regulatory frameworks, which may be complicated in a distant situation.

- **Strategy:** Collaborate with legal specialists well-versed in the jurisdictions concerned. Leverage technology to enable safe and compliant document exchange, electronic signatures, and adherence to regulatory standards in distant transactions.

5. Technology Integration and Adoption:

- **Challenge:** Embracing new technology and ensuring its smooth integration into the deal-making process may be difficult.

- **Strategy:** Provide thorough training and assistance to all parties engaged. Invest in user-friendly tools that allow collaboration, document sharing, and virtual meetings. Regularly update and improve technological solutions to meet developing industry requirements.

6. Security and Privacy Concerns:

- **Challenge:** The virtual aspect of deal-making raises worries about the security and privacy of critical information.

- **Strategy:** Implement rigorous cybersecurity measures, including encrypted communication channels, secure document-sharing platforms, and adherence to industry-standard security regulations. Educate all parties involved on recommended practices for ensuring data security.

7. Cultural Sensitivities:

- **Challenge:** Dealing with varied cultural backgrounds remotely might lead to misunderstandings and possible tensions.

- **Strategy:** Foster cultural intelligence among transaction participants. Conduct cultural awareness training and promote open discussion to address any cultural disparities. Adapt communication techniques to fit cultural sensitivity.

Strategies for Success in Remote Deal-Making

1. Invest in Relationship Building:

- Prioritize relationship-building efforts via virtual networking events, webinars, and collaborative platforms. Foster a feeling of community among deal participants to improve trust and teamwork.

2. Utilize Advanced Virtual Tools:

- Leverage cutting-edge virtual technologies such as augmented reality (AR) and virtual reality (VR) for immersive property experiences. Explore virtual deal rooms and secure document-sharing tools to boost productivity.

3. Create Standard Operating Procedures (SOPs):

- Develop thorough SOPs for remote deal-making procedures. Clearly identify roles, duties, and the sequence of tasks to maintain consistency and efficiency across transactions.

4. Establish Contingency Plans:

- Anticipate possible issues and establish contingency strategies. This includes managing technology malfunctions, communication breakdowns, or unanticipated legal concerns that may develop during the remote deal-making process.

5. Encourage Collaboration and Feedback:

- Foster a collaborative atmosphere by inviting input from all stakeholders. Regularly collect information to identify areas for improvement and enhance the overall distant deal-making experience.

While distant deal-making has its share of hurdles, preemptive methods, and a tech-savvy approach may convert these barriers into possibilities. Successful remote deal-making involves a mix of good communication, technology innovation, cultural knowledge, and a dedication to creating and sustaining trust in the virtual domain. By adopting these tactics, real estate professionals can traverse the distant terrain with confidence and unleash new potential for development and success in the digital era.

Closing Deals with Confidence

Closing a real estate purchase is the conclusion of diligent preparation, good communication, and clever bargaining. The process needs confidence, not only in your property or investment but also in your ability to handle complexity and bring deals to a successful end. In this detailed book, we analyze the main aspects that contribute to completing agreements with confidence in the dynamic world of real estate.

1. Mastering the Art of Communication:

Building Rapport:

Establishing a good connection with customers and stakeholders is the cornerstone of confident deal-closing. Actively listen to their needs, problems, and objectives. Tailor your message to connect with their objectives, establishing trust in your comprehension and dedication.

Clear and Transparent Communication:

Clarity creates confidence. Clearly clarify terms, expectations, and deadlines. Transparency regarding the process and anticipated hurdles develop trust, a critical component in confident deal-closing.

2. Negotiating with Authority:

Preparation is Key:

Confidence in negotiating originates from good preparation. Understand the market, grasp your client's stance, and anticipate probable objections. Armed with information, you may negotiate from a position of power and aggressiveness.

Creative Problem Solving:

Approach talks with a problem-solving approach. Be open to new ideas that benefit all parties. Confidence in your capacity to identify mutually beneficial results adds to a successful deal conclusion.

3. Leveraging Technology and Data:

Utilizing Real-time Data:

In the digital era, data is a tremendous instrument. Leverage real-time market data to help your discussions. Being equipped with precise information instills confidence, portraying you as a competent and trustworthy expert.

Virtual Tools for Virtual Confidence:

In an age of distant deals, virtual tools and platforms play a key role. Virtual tours, augmented reality, and digital documentation not only speed operations but also boost your ability to present and close business with confidence, even from a distance.

4. Building and Maintaining Trust:

Establishing Credibility:

Confidence is directly tied to believability. Showcase your skills with a strong internet presence, customer testimonials, and a track record of successful negotiations.

This establishes trust, a crucial aspect in completing agreements with confidence.

Consistent Communication:

Maintain regular and proactive communication throughout the deal-making process.

Regular updates, fast replies, and an open flow of information enhance trust, enabling all parties to continue with confidence.

5. Overcoming Objections with Grace:

Addressing Concerns Head-on:

Confident deal-closing entails handling concerns with elegance and knowledge. Anticipate future issues and aggressively give solutions.

A confident reaction to concerns reassures customers and helps easier transactions.

Adaptive Negotiation:

Confidence is not about being rigid but adjusting to situations with composure. Be open to concessions, and alternate ideas, and overcome unanticipated roadblocks with a calm and confident approach

6. Closing the Deal:

Timely and Efficient Processes:

Confidence in deal-closing is heightened by efficient procedures. Ensure that documentation is in order, deadlines are fulfilled, and all legal elements are thoroughly addressed. A shortened closure procedure instills trust in all parties.

Celebrating Success:

Acknowledge and celebrate the successful conclusion of transactions. This not only enhances team morale but also strengthens the faith of customers in your capacity to generate excellent results.

Closing transactions with confidence is an art that involves communication finesse, negotiating power, technology insight, and a dedication to developing and sustaining trust. As a real estate agent, honing these talents assures not just the success of individual transactions but also the long-term development and reputation of your firm. Approach each transaction with a sense of purpose, equipped with information, and radiate the confidence that converts problems into chances for success in the ever-evolving world of real estate.

CHAPTER 6

LEGAL AND COMPLIANCE CONSIDERATIONS UNVEILED

In the delicate dance of real estate transactions, the attention typically falls on the legal and regulatory issues that underlie every sale. As real estate professionals weave through the complexity of property transfers, ownership changes, and contractual agreements, a comprehensive awareness of the legal environment becomes vital. This part of our comprehensive book acts as a compass, leading practitioners through the diverse area of legal and compliance matters, assuring not only legitimate interactions but also ethical and frictionless transactions.

1. The Legal Framework of Real Estate Transactions

Understanding Legal Fundamentals:

Real estate transactions depend on a foundation of legal concepts. This section discusses the underlying ideas controlling property transfers, ownership rights, and contractual duties. From the principles of property law to the subtleties of contractual enforceability, a solid grasp of legal fundamentals creates the framework for successful transactions.

Roles of Legal Professionals:

Legal experts play crucial roles in real estate transactions. This section unravels the roles of lawyers, title firms, and other legal specialists. Their duties, from due diligence to contract reviews, are deconstructed to give a thorough knowledge of how legal expertise impacts the direction of a business.

2. Legal Documentation and Contracts

Drafting Airtight Contracts:

Crafting a solid real estate contract is an art. This section digs into the complexities of constructing airtight agreements, addressing the crucial factors that safeguard the interests of all parties involved. From terms and conditions to contingencies, knowing the subtleties of contract writing is vital to successful and legally sound agreements.

Navigating Purchase Agreements:

Purchase agreements serve as the cornerstone of real estate transactions. This section navigates the legal ramifications of purchase agreements, offering light on what makes these contracts legally binding and enforceable. From offer to acceptance, each step is scrutinized to guarantee a complete grasp of the legal forces at play.

Contingencies and Escrow:

Contingencies and escrow add levels of legal sophistication to transactions. This section discusses the legal concerns regarding contingencies in contracts and the safe management of monies in escrow. Understanding these legal procedures is crucial for both the buyer and the seller to traverse the transaction route with confidence.

3. Regulatory Compliance in Real Estate

Fair Housing Laws and Anti-Discrimination Regulations:

Fair housing legislation and anti-discrimination policies alter the ethical environment of real estate deals. This section scrutinizes the legal requirements regarding fair housing and anti-discrimination, ensuring that real estate professionals act within the confines of law and ethics.

Environmental Regulations:

As environmental awareness develops, so does the attention to environmental rules in real estate. This section analyzes the legal landscape of environmental factors, spanning evaluations, disclosures, and conformity to regulatory norms. An awareness of these standards is vital for navigating a landscape increasingly focused on sustainable and ethical behaviors.

Zoning Laws and Land Use Regulations:

Zoning rules and land use restrictions exercise enormous influence over real estate transactions. This section unravels the legal ramifications of zoning rules, analyzing how they affect land usage and development. Compliance with municipal legislation becomes a critical factor for real estate brokers navigating the legal environment.

4. Legal Due Diligence and Disclosures

Due Diligence Processes:

Due diligence is a cornerstone of legal and informed real estate purchases. This section dives into the legal procedures related to due diligence, offering insights into the duties and obligations of all parties involved. Thorough due diligence is not merely a recommended practice; it is a legal duty.

Mandatory Disclosures:

Legal standards for reporting important information are non-negotiable in real estate. This section addresses the responsibility of real estate professionals to provide mandated disclosures. Understanding what must be reported, and when, is crucial to ensuring legal integrity throughout the transaction process.

5. Handling Legal Challenges and Disputes

Resolution of Disputes:

Despite thorough preparation, disagreements might develop. There are ways to settle conflicts in a legally sound manner. Whether via mediation, arbitration, or litigation, knowing the legal methods for conflict resolution is crucial to navigating problems with confidence.

Litigation in Real Estate:

When problems worsen, legal action may be unavoidable. This section gives insights into the legal implications of litigation in real estate. Understanding the procedures involved, from filing a lawsuit to court hearings, prepares real estate professionals to negotiate the legal environment with grace.

6. Staying Updated on Legal Changes

Adapting to Legislative Changes:

Real estate law is a changing terrain. This section covers techniques for remaining updated about changes in the legal system. Adapting to legislative adjustments ensures that real estate professionals work within the confines of existing and growing legal norms.

Professional Development in Legal Competence:

Ongoing professional growth is the cornerstone of legal competence. This section investigates ways for real estate professionals to better their grasp of legal matters. Continuing education ensures that practitioners stay at the forefront of legal knowledge and skill.

Navigating Virtual Wholesaling Regulations

In the ever-evolving face of real estate, the introduction of virtual wholesaling has opened new possibilities for entrepreneurs seeking profitable prospects. However, the virtual sphere comes with its own set of restrictions and issues that knowledgeable real estate agents must negotiate to maintain legitimate and ethical operations. This detailed study covers the complicated web of virtual wholesaling rules, giving a blueprint for companies wishing to prosper in the digital economy

1. The Regulatory Landscape of Virtual Wholesaling

Federal Regulations:

Virtual wholesaling doesn't insulate businesses from federal real estate restrictions. Compliance with legislation such as the Fair Housing Act, which forbids discrimination, and adherence to federal disclosure standards are crucial. Entrepreneurs must manage these government laws, assuring ethical interactions in the virtual environment.

State-Specific Regulations:

Real estate is essentially local, and restrictions may vary greatly from state to state. Understanding the particular needs of each target market is vital. State rules influence licensing, contract structures, and disclosure duties. Entrepreneurs involved in virtual wholesaling must rigorously examine and adhere to the legislation in the states where they operate.

2. Navigating Licensing Requirements

Real Estate Licensing:

While virtual wholesaling doesn't usually entail the actual purchase or selling of assets, licensing requirements might still apply. Some states may need real estate licenses for operations linked to wholesaling, particularly if specific conditions are satisfied. Entrepreneurs must carefully assess the licensing environment to guarantee compliance with state rules.

Brokerage Considerations:

In virtual wholesaling, entrepreneurs typically operate as intermediates, linking vendors with buyers. Understanding the subtleties of brokerage rules and regulations is crucial. In several places, functioning as a real estate broker without appropriate licensure is unlawful. Entrepreneurs must evaluate if their virtual wholesaling operations mistakenly come inside the definition of brokerage and take appropriate actions to comply.

3. Compliance with Marketing Regulations

Digital Marketing Standards:

Virtual wholesaling mainly depends on digital marketing tactics to reach a bigger audience.

However, enterprises must conform to digital marketing norms and rules. Compliance with privacy laws, anti-spam rules, and ethical marketing practices is crucial to avoid legal hazards.

Transparent Dealings:

Transparency is a cornerstone of ethical virtual wholesaling. Entrepreneurs must give precise and clear information about the assets they are promoting. Misrepresentation or omission to disclose important data might lead to legal ramifications.

4. Data Security and Privacy Concerns

Secure Handling of Data:

In the virtual environment, data security is crucial. Entrepreneurs must establish rigorous cybersecurity procedures to preserve sensitive information. Compliance with data protection rules, such as the General Data Protection Regulation (GDPR) for international transactions, assures the ethical management of customer and transaction data.

Privacy Policies and Disclosures:

Entrepreneurs engaging in virtual wholesaling should design and openly show privacy rules. Clear disclosures regarding how data is gathered, processed, and kept create trust and reflect a commitment to privacy compliance.

5. Adapting to Emerging Regulations

Technology Integration:

As technology advances, so do rules. Entrepreneurs must keep current with changing technology and the regulatory revisions that follow them. From blockchain in transactions to artificial intelligence in market research, knowing the legal ramifications of cutting-edge technology is vital.

<u>Continuous Learning and Compliance:</u>

A commitment to constant learning is vital for businesses negotiating virtual wholesaling restrictions. Staying updated about regulatory changes, participating in industry seminars, and connecting with legal experts are tactics to maintain continuing compliance.

Negotiating virtual wholesaling restrictions is a vital component of developing a viable and ethical real estate company. Entrepreneurs must approach the virtual environment with a solid awareness of federal and state rules, licensing requirements, marketing standards, and data security commitments. Compliance isn't only a legal obligation; it's a basis for creating trust and credibility in the virtual economy. By accepting laws and adjusting to the developing legal environment, businesses may position themselves for success and sustainability in the dynamic world of virtual wholesaling.

Ensuring Compliance in Cross-Border Transactions

As the global real estate industry continues to develop, cross-border transactions have become more frequent, enabling chances for investors to explore new markets and profit from foreign property investments. However, given the intricacies of multiple legal systems, regulatory frameworks, and cultural subtleties, maintaining compliance in cross-border transactions is crucial. This book presents an in-depth analysis of the concerns, problems, and methods for navigating the regulatory environment and achieving legal conformance in the arena of cross-border real estate transactions.

1. Understanding the Cross-Border Landscape

Diverse Legal Systems:

One of the key obstacles in cross-border transactions is the variety of legal systems. Each nation has its unique set of laws regulating real estate transactions, from property rights to contractual duties. Investors must educate themselves with the legal framework of the target nation to guarantee compliance at every step of the transaction.

Cultural and Regulatory Nuances:

Beyond legal frameworks, cultural and regulatory subtleties play a key role in cross-border transactions. Understanding local cultures, business practices, and regulatory quirks is vital. This involves understanding special rules pertaining to property ownership, finance, and tax ramifications in individual countries.

Key Considerations for Compliance:

Legal Due Diligence:

Thorough legal due diligence is the cornerstone of compliance in cross-border transactions. Investors must perform a detailed study of the legal requirements of the target nation. This involves comprehending property laws, zoning requirements, and any limits on foreign ownership.

Contractual Agreements:

Crafting effective contractual agreements is crucial. Contracts should be properly prepared to meet the legal requirements of both the buyer's and seller's countries. Attention to precision in terminology, terms, and conditions assures enforceability and compliance on a worldwide scale.

Tax Implications:

Tax issues are crucial in cross-border transactions. Investors need to be aware of tax responsibilities in both the home nation and the target jurisdiction. This includes comprehending any relevant capital gains taxes, stamp duties, or other levies that may affect the transaction.

Foreign Investment Regulations:

Many nations have unique restrictions regarding foreign investment in real estate. Compliance with these standards is vital to prevent legal difficulties. Investors must be aware of any limitations, permissions, or reporting requirements imposed by the target nation on foreign real estate transactions.

2. Navigating Regulatory Challenges

Legal Expertise:

Engaging local legal knowledge is a sensible method for addressing regulatory hurdles. Collaborating with attorneys who specialize in real estate transactions in the target nation gives vital insights into local laws and regulatory peculiarities.

Legal specialists may help investors through the difficulties, assuring compliance at every stage.

Cultural Competence:

Cultural competency is an often neglected part of compliance. Understanding the cultural environment in which transactions occur is vital for creating healthy connections and overcoming possible legal hazards. Respect for local traditions and business etiquette helps to the success of cross-border dealings.

3. Leveraging Technology for Compliance

Digital Platforms and Tools:

Technology plays a significant role in guaranteeing compliance in cross-border transactions. Digital platforms and solutions expedite paperwork, promote secure communication, and give real-time updates on regulatory requirements.

Utilizing technology boosts productivity and decreases the danger of neglecting regulatory duties.

Data Security and Privacy:

Given the transnational nature of cross-border transactions, data security and privacy compliance are crucial. Investors must comply with worldwide data protection regulations, such as the General Data Protection Regulation (GDPR), to preserve sensitive information and guarantee compliance with international privacy laws.

Maintaining compliance in cross-border real estate transactions is a multidimensional task that involves a profound awareness of legal, cultural, and regulatory contexts. Investors moving into overseas markets must emphasize legal due diligence, establish thorough contractual agreements, and keep aware of tax consequences and foreign investment rules.

Collaboration with local legal professionals and a dedication to cultural competency help to effective and compliant transactions.

In the digital age, employing technology becomes not only a convenience but a need for effective compliance management. By embracing the intricacies of cross-border transactions and proactively tackling regulatory barriers, real estate investors may develop a foundation for success in the global economy.

Mitigating Risks in the Virtual Realm of Real Estate

As the real estate sector undergoes a digital transformation, the virtual world brings both extraordinary prospects and a distinct set of obstacles. From virtual wholesaling to online markets and distant deal-making, real estate professionals must traverse the digital world with diligence to reduce hazards efficiently. This thorough book digs into the techniques and considerations required for managing hazards in the virtual environment, guaranteeing a safe and profitable journey into the digital future of real estate.

Understanding Virtual Real Estate Risk

Cybersecurity Threats:

In the virtual environment, cybersecurity dangers loom big. Real estate transactions contain huge volumes of sensitive data, making them great targets for hackers. Mitigating threats needs comprehensive cybersecurity measures, including encryption, secure communication routes, and frequent cybersecurity assessments.

Data Privacy Concerns:

Data privacy is a fundamental feature of virtual interactions. The collecting, storage, and exchange of personal and financial information demands compliance with data protection standards. Real estate professionals must create strong data privacy rules, educate stakeholders, and deploy secure platforms to limit the dangers associated with data breaches.

Transaction Integrity:

Maintaining the integrity of virtual transactions is a key problem. Risks such as fraud, deception, and illegal access may weaken the trust of virtual trades. Implementing safe transaction protocols, doing rigorous due diligence, and leveraging blockchain technology for transaction transparency are techniques to reduce these risks.

Key Strategies for Mitigating Virtual Real Estate Risks

Educating Stakeholders:

Mitigating dangers in the virtual domain starts with educating all parties involved. From customers to team members, raising knowledge about possible dangers, cybersecurity best practices, and adherence to compliance requirements is vital. Well-informed stakeholders operate as the first line of defense against virtual dangers.

Implementing Secure Technologies:

The choice of technology utilized in virtual real estate transactions greatly affects risk minimization. Employing secure communication tools, encrypted platforms, and cutting-edge cybersecurity solutions fortifies the virtual environment. Regularly upgrading and patching IT infrastructure is crucial to keep ahead of new risks.

Comprehensive Due Diligence:

Thorough due diligence is a cornerstone of risk reduction in every real estate transaction, virtual or otherwise. Virtual trades should receive the same rigorous examination as conventional ones. This involves confirming property facts, reviewing legal papers, and evaluating the reliability of all involved parties.

Legal Compliance and Documentation:

Adhering to legal compliance norms is non-negotiable in the virtual domain. Real estate agents must guarantee that all virtual transactions conform with local and international legislation. Robust documentation methods, including clear contracts and disclosure statements, help with legal compliance and risk minimization.

Risk Mitigation in Virtual Wholesaling

Transparent Dealings:

In virtual wholesaling, openness is crucial. Mitigating risks entails giving accurate and clear information about properties, appraisals, and transaction structures. Transparent interactions establish confidence and lessen the possibility of conflicts or legal difficulties.

Secure Virtual Communication:

Virtual wholesaling requires significant digital communication. Implementing secure communication channels, encrypted emails, and virtual conferencing solutions with robust cybersecurity capabilities preserves important information. Communication security is crucial to reducing hazards in virtual wholesaling.

Adapting to Regulatory Changes:

The regulatory environment in virtual wholesaling is evolving. Mitigating risks demands being current with developments in real estate legislation, digital transaction restrictions, and compliance requirements. Entrepreneurs must change their virtual wholesaling practices to line with growing regulatory obligations.

Reducing risks in the virtual arena of real estate involves a proactive and planned strategy. Cybersecurity awareness, data protection safeguards, rigorous due diligence, and legal compliance are essential pillars of risk reduction. Real estate professionals must embrace secure technology, educate stakeholders, and adapt to the developing regulatory framework to cross the digital frontier with confidence. By prioritizing risk mitigation techniques, the sector can embrace the tremendous potential of the virtual world while ensuring the integrity and security of real estate transactions in the digital age.

CHAPTER 7

CRAFTING A VIRTUAL WHOLESALING BRAND

In the dynamic domain of real estate, virtual wholesaling has arisen as a disruptive technique, breaking down geographical constraints and using the power of the digital environment. Crafting a virtual wholesaling brand needs a deliberate combination of digital marketing, branding concepts, and a thorough grasp of the specific intricacies of the virtual marketplace. This in-depth examination digs into the important parts of developing and improving a virtual wholesaling brand, delivering insights and effective tactics for success in the digital frontier of real estate.

Defining the Essence of a Virtual Wholesaling Brand

Crafting a virtual wholesaling brand starts with a comprehensive grasp of the virtual marketplace. Virtual wholesaling includes the purchase and disposal of real estate assets utilizing digital tools and platforms, liberating practitioners from the restrictions of physical presence. This knowledge creates the basis upon which a compelling brand may be constructed.

Brand Values and Unique Selling Propositions

In the digital world, a brand is more than simply a logo or a name; it is the embodiment of values and a distinct value proposition. Virtual wholesalers must identify their brand values, integrity, transparency, efficiency and describe what sets them distinct in the virtual realm. This clarity is the foundation for building a brand identity that connects with the target audience.

Crafting Visual Branding Elements for Virtual Wholesaling

The Power of Visual Identity:

In the virtual sphere, where initial impressions are typically established at a look, visual aspects play a key role. Crafting a memorable logo, choosing a consistent color palette, and building an aesthetically attractive website are key parts of establishing a strong visual brand identity. These components add to brand awareness and generate a feeling of professionalism in the virtual wholesaling sector.

Optimizing Website Design for User Experience:

A virtual wholesaling brand's digital shop is its website. Ensuring a fluid and user-friendly experience is crucial. From straightforward navigation to mobile adaptability, the website must be tailored to give a favorable user experience.

Clear calls-to-action and readily available content boost the website's efficacy in turning visitors into leads.

Leveraging Social Media in Virtual Wholesaling Branding

Choosing the Right Platforms:

Social media is a fantastic instrument for virtual wholesaling branding. Identifying the most appropriate channels, such as LinkedIn, Facebook, or Instagram, helps practitioners to engage with a bigger audience. Each site has its benefits, and a smart approach to social media selection enables effective brand marketing.

Content Creation for Engagement:

Content is the money of the digital universe. Crafting engaging content, whether via instructive blog articles, visually attractive infographics, or intriguing video content, promotes a company as an expert in virtual wholesaling. Educational material that addresses the pain points of prospective customers creates trust and promotes the business as a valued resource in the industry.

Implementing SEO Strategies for Virtual Wholesaling Brand Visibility

Optimizing for Search Engines:

Visibility is vital in the digital realm, and search engine optimization (SEO) is the key to online discoverability. Implementing SEO tactics guarantees that a virtual wholesaling brand appears highly in search engine results, boosting organic traffic and improving brand exposure.

Utilizing Keywords for Targeted Reach:

Keyword optimization is a cornerstone of efficient SEO. Understanding the keywords and phrases prospective customers use when looking for virtual wholesaling services enables firms to adapt their web material for optimum exposure.

Targeted keyword integration across digital assets boosts the brand's reach to a relevant audience.

Building Trust Through Transparent Communication

Transparency as a Brand Pillar:

Trust is the backbone of every successful brand. In virtual wholesaling, when transactions occur remotely, transparency becomes even more crucial. Clearly describing procedures, offering honest information about agreements, and being candid about possible obstacles assist in the creation of confidence in the virtual wholesaling brand.

Client Testimonials and Success Stories:

Real-world success stories and customer testimonials are essential tools for generating trust. Featuring testimonials on the website and sharing success stories via digital media humanizes the business and illustrates its capacity to provide concrete outcomes in virtual wholesale transactions.

Innovative Technologies and Brand Adaptability

Embracing Technological Innovations:

Virtual wholesaling occurs at the crossroads of real estate and technology. Brands that adopt novel technology, such as virtual reality (VR) for property tours or artificial intelligence (AI) for data analysis, display versatility and a forward-thinking strategy. Integrating these technologies into branding initiatives puts the brand as a leader in the virtual wholesaling arena.

Brand Adaptability in a Dynamic Landscape:

The internet world is changing, and virtual wholesaling companies must be agile. Staying educated about developing trends, promptly embracing new technology, and modifying branding tactics in reaction to market developments shows a brand's ability to traverse the ever-evolving virtual landscape.

Building a virtual wholesaling brand is a delicate process that involves a thorough awareness of the digital market, a dedication to openness, and a purposeful balance of visual and content aspects. By defining brand values, optimizing visual and digital assets, leveraging social media effectively, and staying adaptable to technological innovations, virtual wholesaling brands can not only establish a strong online presence but also foster trust and credibility in the competitive world of remote real estate transactions. Mastering the art of virtual wholesaling branding is not just about developing a logo or a website; it's about constructing a digital identity that connects with customers, sets the company apart, and positions it as a leader in the new frontier of virtual wholesaling.

Effective Online Marketing Strategies

In the fast-paced and linked world of the internet, effective online marketing techniques are important for organizations trying to prosper and stay competitive. This comprehensive book analyzes a plethora of strategies, methods, and best practices that organizations may implement to harness the power of the digital environment, connect with their target audience, and produce practical outcomes in the online arena.

Digital Transformation and Consumer Behavior

The digital world has experienced a fundamental upheaval, changing how customers find, connect with, and make purchase choices. Understanding the changes in customer behavior is crucial to establishing online marketing techniques that connect with the current audience.

The Multichannel Approach:

Effective Internet marketing extends beyond a single channel. The multichannel method entails carefully integrating multiple online channels such as social media, search engines, email, and content marketing to build a unified and compelling online presence. Each channel performs a specific function in the consumer experience, from awareness to conversion.

Key Components of Effective Online Marketing Strategies

Search Engine Optimization (SEO):

SEO is a cornerstone of internet presence. Businesses must optimize their digital assets, including websites and content, to rank better in search engine results. By aligning with relevant keywords and delivering excellent content, companies boost their chances of being found by prospective consumers.

Content Marketing Excellence:

Content is the money of the internet. Crafting high-quality, relevant, and helpful content develops authority, engages the audience, and promotes organic traffic. Whether via blog posts, videos, infographics, or podcasts, a solid content marketing plan is crucial to online marketing success.

Social Media Mastery:

Social media platforms are strong tools for generating brand recognition and promoting engagement. Effective online marketing entails picking the correct social media platforms for the target audience, developing shareable content, and participating in meaningful conversations to establish a devoted online community.

Email Marketing Strategies:

Despite the growth of multiple communication channels, email marketing remains a vital tool for organizations. Building and maintaining an email list enables direct engagement with the audience. Personalized and targeted email marketing may generate conversions and build continuing client connections.

Strategies for Effective Online Advertising

Paid Search Advertising (PPC):

Paid search advertising, frequently via platforms like Google Ads, allows companies to compete for ad placement in search engine results. This tailored method guarantees that advertising is presented to visitors actively seeking related items or services, boosting the possibility of conversions.

Social Media Advertising:

Platforms like Facebook, Instagram, and LinkedIn provide powerful advertising choices. Social media advertising enables firms to target certain demographics, interests, and behaviors, reaching a highly targeted audience. Compelling pictures and engaging ad language are important for success in social media advertising.

Remarketing and Retargeting:

Remarketing and retargeting entail reaching out to people who have previously connected with a brand online. Whether via website visits or abandoned shopping carts, this method maintains the brand in front of prospective buyers, boosting the odds of conversion upon a repeat visit.

Harnessing Data for Informed Decision-Making

Data Analytics and Performance Measurement:

Effective web marketing depends on data-driven insights. Utilizing technologies like Google Analytics, firms may assess the efficacy of their online marketing initiatives. Key indicators such as website traffic, conversion rates, and user behavior give essential information for enhancing strategy.

A/B Testing for Optimization:

A/B testing entails experimenting with variants of web pieces, such as ad content, landing sites, or email subject lines, to see which works better. This iterative method enables organizations to adapt their strategy based on real-time data, optimizing for maximum effect.

Cultivating a Positive Online Reputation

Online Reputation Management:

Building and keeping a great internet reputation is crucial. Businesses must regularly monitor internet reviews, react to client comments, and handle problems swiftly. A good internet reputation promotes trust and trustworthiness, affecting purchase choices.

Authenticity and Brand Consistency:

Consistency in branding across online media is vital for gaining trust. From visual aspects to message, preserving authenticity and consistency promotes an identifiable brand identity. Consumers are more inclined to connect with and trust businesses that regularly convey a coherent message.

Adapting to Emerging Trends and Technologies

Embracing Technological Innovations:

Staying ahead in internet marketing entails adopting evolving technology. From artificial intelligence in chatbots to virtual and augmented reality experiences, organizations must examine and integrate technologies that connect with their objectives and improve the consumer experience.

Voice Search Optimization:

With the proliferation of speech-activated devices, optimizing for voice search is increasingly crucial. Businesses should adjust their online content to fit natural language inquiries, assuring exposure in the developing world of voice search.

Efficient Internet marketing techniques are crucial for organizations hoping to prosper in the digital world. By understanding the dynamic online world, mastering essential components like SEO, content marketing, and social media, and utilizing the power of data, companies can connect with their audience, generate engagement, and achieve demonstrable success. With a dedication to adaptation, a focus on customer experience, and an acceptance of new technology, companies can traverse the digital future with confidence, maintaining their relevance and effect in the ever-evolving world of online marketing.

Leveraging Social Media for Real Estate Success

In the ever-evolving market of real estate, harnessing social media has become a vital approach to success. Social media platforms provide a vibrant and important environment for real estate agents to engage with customers, display properties, and develop a strong online presence. This thorough book analyzes the numerous facets of social media marketing, giving insights and specific actions for real estate success in the digital environment.

Understanding the Impact of Social Media on Real Estate

The Shift in Consumer Behavior:

The emergence of social media has radically impacted how users interact with information, make choices, and connect with companies. In the real estate context, prospective buyers and sellers use platforms like Facebook, Instagram, and LinkedIn to explore properties, gain data, and communicate with real estate experts.

Visual Storytelling and Property Showcase:

Social media's visual nature combines neatly with the real estate industry's requirement for appealing imagery. Real estate agents may harness platforms to display homes via high-quality photographs, virtual tours, and compelling films.

Visual storytelling captivates audiences and increases interest in listed properties.

Crafting a Strategic Social Media Presence

Choosing the Right Platforms:

Each social media network caters to a specific audience and content type. Real estate agents must intentionally pick platforms that correspond with their target audience. Instagram may be perfect for visually attractive property photographs, while LinkedIn gives a professional platform for networking and industry updates.

Building a Consistent Brand Identity:

Consistency is crucial in social media branding. Real estate professionals should maintain a coherent brand identity across channels, including consistent images, messages, and tone. A unified brand presence creates familiarity and encourages confidence among prospective customers.

Social Media Content Strategies for Real Estate

Educational Content and Market Insights:

Positioning oneself as an industry expert includes giving instructional information and market insights. Real estate experts may write blog entries, infographics, or films detailing market trends, investment methods, and relevant insights. This material not only demonstrates skill but also delivers value to the viewer.

Property Showcasing and Virtual Tours:

Harnessing the visual appeal of social media, real estate agents may display homes via visually attractive postings and virtual tours. Platforms like Instagram and Facebook allow for immersive property experiences, enabling prospective purchasers to explore listings online.

Client Testimonials and Success Stories:

Sharing customer testimonials and success stories gives a personal touch to social media presence. Positive experiences from prior customers act as compelling recommendations and develop a reputation. These tales humanize the real estate agent and build an emotional connection with the audience.

Engagement and Community Building

Two-Way Communication:

Social media is a venue for conversation. Real estate agents should actively connect with their audience by replying to comments, addressing queries, and engaging in conversations. This two-way contact develops a feeling of community and displays the professional as accessible and responsive.

Hosting Live Events and Q&A Sessions:

Live events and Q&A sessions on platforms like Instagram Live or Facebook Live allow real-time engagement. Real estate professionals may hold virtual open houses, Q&A sessions about the local market, or conversations on industry trends. Live events boost engagement and allow for direct connection with the audience.

Advertising and Targeted Campaigns

Paid Advertising on Social Media:

Paid advertising on social media enables real estate agents to target certain demographics, ensuring their material reaches the most appropriate audience. Platforms like Facebook Ads and Instagram Ads provide accurate targeting based on geography, demographics, and interests, boosting the effect of marketing efforts.

Retargeting Strategies:

Retargeting entails reaching out to those who have previously interacted with a real estate professional's material. This method maintains the brand at the forefront of prospective customers' thoughts, improving the possibility of conversion. Retargeting advertising might feature fresh listings, highlight success stories, or give helpful material.

Measuring Success and Iterative Improvement

Analytics and Key Performance Indicators (KPIs):

Real estate agents should leverage social media analytics tools to monitor the efficacy of their efforts. Tracking important metrics such as engagement rates, reach, and conversion rates gives vital insights into the efficacy of the social media strategy. Analyzing data enables iterative improvements and optimization.

A/B Testing for Content Optimization:

Experimenting with various kinds of content via A/B testing helps real estate agents determine what connects most with their audience. Testing changes in graphics, descriptions, or publishing schedules helps enhance the content strategy for best interaction.

Navigating Challenges and Staying Relevant

Navigating Regulatory Compliance:

Real estate agents must negotiate industry restrictions and legal issues while utilizing social media. Adhering to fair housing regulations, providing correct property information, and guaranteeing compliance with ethical standards are crucial for preserving a good reputation and avoiding legal complications.

Adaptation to Emerging Trends:

Staying relevant in the changing social media ecosystem means responding to evolving trends. Real estate agents should follow industry advancements, investigate new features on social media platforms, and embrace creative technology like augmented reality for virtual property tours.

Harnessing social media is a dynamic and complex method for attaining success in the real estate sector. By proactively developing a strong social media presence, providing interesting content, cultivating community, and deploying targeted advertising, real estate agents can connect with their audience, showcase properties, and establish lasting connections.

CHAPTER 8

SCALING YOUR VIRTUAL WHOLESALING BUSINESS

Scaling a company is a difficult and dynamic process that demands careful planning, smart execution, and the capacity to duplicate success on a greater scale. Whether you're a startup wanting to expand or an established organization striving for considerable development, implementing efficient scaling tactics is vital. This thorough book discusses essential ideas and concrete actions for reproducing success and developing your company to new heights.

Understanding the Essence of Scaling

Defining Scaling in Business:

Scaling goes beyond simply expansion; it requires boosting your business's ability to manage growth effectively. It's about reproducing the characteristics that led to your early success on a bigger scale, preserving quality, and fulfilling growing demands without sacrificing performance.

The Role of Replication:

Replication is a major concept in scalability. It entails copying successful procedures, tactics, and systems that have proved beneficial in a smaller setting. Replicating success enables firms to retain consistency and create sustainable development.

Foundational Elements for Successful Scaling

Clear Business Model and Value Proposition:

Before increasing, verify your company strategy is clear and successful. Define your unique value proposition and understand what makes your firm distinct. A firm foundation ensures that scaling initiatives grow atop a stable framework.

Efficient Systems and Processes:

Efficiency is crucial to growth. Streamline and improve your current systems and procedures. Identifying opportunities for automation and creating standardized procedures guarantees that your organization can manage greater volume without losing quality.

Scaling Your Market Presence

Market Research and Expansion:

Conduct detailed market research to find possible growth prospects. Understand the demographics, tastes, and trends in new markets. Tailor your strategy to each location, realizing that what works in one place may require tweaks elsewhere.

Strategic Partnerships and Alliances:

Form strategic alliances with firms that complement yours. These relationships may give access to new markets, resources, and expertise. A collaborative approach supports reciprocal progress and magnifies your scaling efforts.

Leveraging Technology for Efficiency

Data-Driven Decision Making:

Harness the power of data analytics to influence your scaling choices. Analyze consumer behavior, market trends, and performance indicators.

Data-driven insights inform strategic decisions and help you adjust to shifting conditions.

Scalable Technology Infrastructure:

Invest in scalable technology that can expand with your firm. Ensure your infrastructure, including software and hardware, can manage rising demands without losing performance. Scalable technology is a cornerstone of effective scalability.

Scaling Marketing and Customer Acquisition

Digital Marketing Strategies:

Extend your digital marketing efforts to reach a bigger audience. Utilize customized advertising, content marketing, and social media to interact with prospective consumers. Leverage search engine optimization (SEO) to boost online exposure and generate organic visitors.

Customer Relationship Management (CRM) Systems:

Implement a strong CRM system to manage customer contacts and simplify communication. A well-designed CRM system enables individualized customer experiences, increases customer retention, and simplifies scalable customer management.

Building a High-Performing Team

Recruitment and Talent Acquisition:

As you expand, concentrate on attracting great talent. Identify people that match your business culture and possess the talents essential for your development trajectory. Building a high-performing team is vital for sustainable success.

Training and Development Programs:

Invest in training and development programs to provide your staff with the skills required for expanded operations.

Continuous learning guarantees that your team adjusts to new problems and adds to the efficiency of scaling initiatives.

Financial Management and Scaling

Financial Planning and Forecasting:

Develop a detailed finance strategy that corresponds with your growing goals. Forecast costs, revenue estimates, and cash flow needs. A good finance plan gives the resources required for effective growth.

Access to finance:

Explore several routes for acquiring finance to help your scaling initiatives. Whether via investors, loans, or other funding sources, having appropriate cash is vital for undertaking scaling projects without sacrificing financial stability.

Measuring Success and Iterative Improvement

Key Performance Indicators (KPIs):

Define and monitor key performance metrics that fit with your scaling objectives. Metrics linked to client acquisition, conversion rates, and revenue growth give insights into the efficacy of your scaling strategy.

Feedback Loops and Adaptability:

Encourage input from consumers, staff, and stakeholders. Establish feedback loops that inform your decision-making process. An adaptive strategy enables you to iterate on your ideas depending on real-time information and changing market circumstances.

Scaling Responsibly and Sustainably

Risk Mitigation methods: Identify possible hazards associated with scaling and execute mitigation methods. Proactively address difficulties linked to operational efficiency, market volatility, and regulatory changes to guarantee a smooth scaling process.

Sustainable Scaling Practices:

Prioritize sustainability in your scaling processes. Avoid fast development without sufficient infrastructure and protections in place. Sustainable scaling helps your firm to develop smoothly while preserving stability and agility.

Building Systems for Sustainable Growth

Sustainable growth is the cornerstone of a healthy firm, and developing sturdy processes is the key to attaining this prolonged development. Businesses that thrive and prosper over the long term are those that can expand without sacrificing efficiency, quality, or the general health of the business. In this thorough book, we dig into the important techniques and practices for developing systems that support sustainable development and catapult your organization to new heights.

Understanding Sustainable Growth

Defining Sustainable Growth:

Sustainable growth entails developing a firm in a manner that is controllable, lucrative, and durable. It goes beyond immediate, short-term results, stressing a balanced strategy that considers the long-term profitability and health of the company.

The Role of Systems in Growth:

Systems constitute the backbone of sustained development. These are the organized procedures, workflows, and techniques that simplify operations, boost efficiency, and build a platform for growth without adding chaos or compromising the quality of goods or services.

Foundational Elements for Building Sustainable Systems

Clear Vision and Mission:

Before creating processes, a firm must have a defined vision and objective. These guiding principles offer the basis for decision-making and strategy creation. Systems are most successful when linked with the main aims of the company.

Understanding Your Market:

A strong grasp of your market is vital. Regular market research helps you to recognize trends, forecast changes, and alter your processes appropriately. Adaptable systems that adjust to market conditions are more likely to contribute to sustained growth.

Efficient Operations and Process Optimization

Streamlined Workflows:

Efficiency is at the core of sustainable systems. Streamlining processes ensures that operations are done with little friction, decreasing the chance of bottlenecks and delays. Analyze current processes to discover opportunities for improvement and optimization.

Automation for Efficiency:

Leverage automation to boost productivity in repetitive and time-consuming processes. Whether it's automating data entry, email marketing, or customer care procedures, automation frees up human resources for more strategic, value-added tasks.

Scalable Technology Infrastructure

Investing in Scalable Technologies:

As your firm expands, so should your IT infrastructure. Choose technology that can expand your operations, from solid enterprise resource planning (ERP) systems to cloud-based options that enable flexibility and scalability.

Cybersecurity for Scalable Systems:

Building sustainable systems needs a heavy focus on cybersecurity. Protecting sensitive data, customer information and intellectual property is vital for retaining confidence and averting interruptions that might limit progress.

Customer-Centric Systems

Effective Customer Relationship Management (CRM):

A customer-centric strategy is crucial for sustained development. Implementing an efficient CRM system helps you to manage client interactions, monitor preferences, and tailor the customer experience. Satisfied clients are more likely to contribute to long-term growth.

Feedback Loops for Continuous Improvement:

Integrate feedback loops into your systems to acquire information from consumers, staff, and stakeholders. This continual input enables incremental changes, ensuring that your systems grow in response to changing demands and expectations.

Building a High-Performing Team

Strategic Recruitment and Onboarding:

Your crew is a vital aspect of your system. Recruit people who not only possess the essential talents but also fit with the values and culture of your firm. Implement extensive onboarding practices to incorporate new team members effortlessly.

Training and Development Programs:

Invest in training and development initiatives to upskill your personnel. A highly qualified staff is better suited to manage the complexity of expanded operations. Continuous learning develops a culture of progress and creativity.

Financial Management and Planning

Strategic Financial Planning:

Sustainable development demands strong financial management. Develop strategic financial strategies that correspond with your development goals.

This involves budgeting, forecasting, and assuring access to money for growth when required.

Risk Management Strategies:

Identify and minimize risks via comprehensive risk management solutions. Addressing possible difficulties, from economic downturns to industry transitions, helps your systems stay robust in the face of unpredictability.

Measuring Success and Iterative Improvement

Key Performance Indicators (KPIs):

Establish specific key performance indicators (KPIs) that fit with your development objectives. Regularly monitor and evaluate these KPIs to determine the performance of your systems. This data-driven strategy enables informed decision-making.

Iterative Improvement and Adaptability:

A culture of constant development is crucial. Encourage your team to discover opportunities for improvement within the current systems. Being flexible and receptive to change guarantees that your systems grow to meet the needs of a changing corporate environment.

Cultivating a Culture of Innovation

Encouraging Creativity and Innovation:

Innovation is a driving factor behind sustainable development. Foster a culture that supports creativity and innovation within your team. Systems that allow for experimentation and adaptability contribute to continued success.

Embracing Emerging Technologies:

Stay aware of developing technology that is important to your business. Embracing advancements such as artificial intelligence, data analytics, and the Internet of Things may boost the capabilities of your systems and position your firm for future success.

Overcoming Challenges in Scaling Virtually

Scaling a virtual firm poses unique issues that demand inventive solutions and smart strategy. While the advantages of virtual scaling, such as enhanced flexibility and access to varied talent, are important, firms must overcome multiple challenges to guarantee a smooth and sustainable development trajectory. In this detailed book, we investigate the particular obstacles connected with growing digitally and give practical advice on overcoming them.

Understanding the Challenges of Virtual Scaling

Communication Barriers:

One of the key obstacles in virtual scaling is overcoming communication constraints. In a remote workplace, the absence of face-to-face contact may lead to misconceptions, misinterpretation, and a feeling of detachment among team members.

Team Collaboration and Cohesion:

Maintaining a cohesive and productive team becomes more tough in a virtual context. Building a strong work culture, encouraging camaraderie, and guaranteeing effective cooperation are essential parts of overcoming this difficulty.

Technology Infrastructure:

Reliable and scalable technical infrastructure is crucial for virtual scaling. Issues like bandwidth restrictions, cybersecurity concerns, and the integration of multiple systems might inhibit flawless operations.

Employee Engagement and Morale:

Keeping workers interested and motivated in a virtual world demands purposeful efforts. The lack of physical closeness may contribute to feelings of isolation, possibly hurting employee morale and overall work satisfaction.

Cultural Adaptation:

Scaling online typically requires overcoming cultural differences, particularly if the firm grows into new locations. Understanding and adapting to varied cultural norms and work styles is vital for coherent and harmonious virtual scaling.

Strategies for Overcoming Virtual Scaling Challenges

Effective Communication Strategies:

Implement clear and transparent communication routes. Utilize a combination of synchronous and asynchronous communication methods to support diverse working styles. Regular video conferences, town halls, and open forums build a feeling of connectedness.

Building a Strong Team Culture:

Establish a strong team culture that transcends physical borders. Invest in team-building activities, virtual social gatherings, and programs that foster cooperation. Recognize and celebrate team successes to increase morale.

<u>Scalable Technology Solutions:</u>

Invest in scalable technological solutions that meet the rising needs of a virtual firm. Regularly examine and improve your technological infrastructure to ensure it can manage rising workloads and changing business demands.

<u>Employee Engagement Initiatives:</u>

Implement staff engagement activities that promote well-being and build a good virtual work environment. Regular check-ins, virtual team-building activities, and staff recognition programs add to a feeling of belonging and drive.

<u>Cultural Awareness and Inclusion:</u>

Promote cultural awareness and inclusivity inside the virtual workplace. Provide training on cultural differences, promote cross-cultural cooperation, and build an atmosphere where varied ideas are appreciated.

Building Leadership Strategies for Virtual Scaling

Adaptive Leadership:

Cultivate flexible leadership that flourishes in a virtual context. Leaders should be proficient at handling change, establishing a healthy virtual culture, and successfully conveying the organization's goals to remote personnel.

Empowering Remote Leadership:

Empower remote leaders with the knowledge and tools essential to manage virtual teams successfully. This covers training on virtual leadership best practices, communication tactics, and conflict resolution in a distant environment.

Data-Driven Decision-Making:

Leverage data-driven decision-making to analyze the efficacy of virtual scaling tactics. Regularly assess key performance indicators (KPIs) relating to team productivity, employee happiness, and overall company success.

Agile Project Management:

Adopt agile project management approaches that promote flexibility and adaptation. Agile approaches help teams adjust rapidly to changing situations, streamline procedures, and constantly enhance virtual operations.

Navigating Legal and Regulatory Challenges

Compliance and Data Security:

Prioritize compliance with data protection legislation and cybersecurity requirements. Implement comprehensive data security measures, perform frequent compliance audits, and verify that virtual operations comply with appropriate regulatory frameworks.

Cross-Border Regulations:

Understand and handle cross-border restrictions while growing virtually into new locations. Work closely with legal professionals to ensure that the firm conforms with local laws, tax rules, and other jurisdiction-specific needs.

Employment Laws in Virtual Settings:

Stay aware of emerging employment rules relating to virtual labor. Consider legal concerns related to remote workforce management, employment contracts, and any jurisdiction-specific regulations for virtual personnel.

Intellectual Property Protection:

Protect intellectual property in a virtual world. Establish explicit rules and processes for securing proprietary information and trade secrets and ensuring that staff are aware of and comply with intellectual property regulations.

Addressing problems in growing digitally involves a proactive and planned strategy. By tackling communication hurdles, emphasizing team cohesiveness, investing in scalable technology, boosting employee engagement, developing adaptable leadership, and managing legal and regulatory difficulties, organizations may prosper in the virtual frontier. Virtual scaling, when addressed wisely and with a dedication to continuous improvement, offers up potential for sustainable expansion, global reach, and a robust business model in the changing terrain of the virtual world.

CHAPTER 9

REAL-LIFE SUCCESS STORIES

Case Studies of Virtual Wholesalers

In the ever-evolving environment of real estate, virtual wholesaling has evolved as a dynamic and efficient way to property transactions. Virtual wholesalers employ technology and internet platforms to locate, negotiate, and finalize transactions remotely, giving a new dimension to classic real estate processes. This chapter covers case studies of virtual wholesalers who have managed the hurdles and seized the possibilities afforded by the digital domain.

1. The Tech-Savvy Innovator:

Background:

John, a seasoned real estate expert, embraced virtual wholesaling to broaden his reach beyond local markets. Leveraging modern data analytics, he spotted rising patterns and attractive prospects in undeveloped locations.

Strategy:

John invested in cutting-edge technologies for market research, employing predictive analytics to find areas with high potential for property appreciation. Virtual tours and 3D models allowed remote property appraisals, enabling him to make educated judgments without physically visiting each location.

Outcome:

By integrating technology with a strategic strategy, John effectively concluded business in numerous states. His tech-savvy approaches not only raised transaction volume but also positioned him as an industry pioneer, drawing a larger network of investors and sellers.

The Collaborative Virtual Team:

Background:

Sarah, an ambitious entrepreneur, developed a remote workforce to allow virtual wholesaling across multiple marketplaces. Her team consisted of individuals with skills in data research, marketing, and negotiating.

Strategy:

Sarah developed a culture of cooperation using virtual communication platforms, providing flawless coordination among team members distributed across multiple time zones. By adopting project management tools and virtual workspace optimization, the team reduced procedures and boosted overall productivity.

Outcome:

The collaborative virtual team strategy enables Sarah to expand her firm swiftly. By utilizing the unique capabilities of her team members, she effectively discovered and concluded business in multiple marketplaces. The efficiency achieved via remote cooperation led to higher profitability and quicker expansion.

3. The Data-Driven Virtual Wholesaler:

Background:

Michael, a data fanatic, saw the importance of information in the virtual wholesaling market. He focused on employing data analytics to find off-market possibilities and improve his deal-making process.

Strategy:

Michael used extensive data sets, including property records, market trends, and historical sales data. By utilizing machine learning algorithms, he constructed predictive models to estimate property prices and discover possible high-yield investments. This data-driven strategy enables him to make strategic choices based on market trends.

Outcome:

Michael's devotion to data-driven decision-making resulted in a high success rate in locating discounted homes. The accuracy of his projections led to a broad portfolio of lucrative partnerships. His achievement emphasized the value of exploiting data as a strategic advantage in virtual wholesaling.

4. The Social Media Maven:

Background:

Emily, a young entrepreneur, understood the value of social media in communicating with prospective sellers and investors. She deliberately leveraged networks like Instagram, Facebook, and LinkedIn to establish her virtual wholesaling company.

Strategy:

Emily developed compelling information, including property highlights, success stories, and instructive material regarding virtual wholesaling. She employed targeted advertising to reach a larger audience, building a brand that connected with both sellers and investors seeking virtual possibilities.

Outcome:

Emily's social media-focused campaign garnered her significant notoriety and a regular stream of leads. Her online presence not only aided deal-making but also positioned her as an expert in the virtual wholesaling field. The result proved the possibility of leveraging social media as a significant tool for networking and deal acquisition.

These case studies demonstrate the different tactics adopted by virtual wholesalers to traverse the digital environment of real estate. Whether through technology innovation, collaborative teamwork, data-driven decision-making, or social media prowess, these entrepreneurs demonstrate that success in virtual wholesaling is attainable through adaptability, strategic thinking, and leveraging the tools available in the digital landscape. As the real estate sector continues to grow, these case studies provide excellent insights for prospective virtual wholesalers seeking inspiration and practical direction on their entrepreneurial path.

Lessons Learned from Successful Virtual Deals

Success in virtual real estate dealings involves a mix of strategic planning, technical expertise, and agility. Examining the lessons gained from people who have thrived in the virtual arena gives significant insights for persons navigating the digital environment of real estate transactions.

1. Embrace Technology as Your Ally

Lesson Learned:

Successful virtual negotiations illustrate the necessity of embracing technology as a vital ally. Virtual wholesalers that harness modern technologies for market study, virtual property appraisals, and communication have a particular edge.

Application:

Invest in technology such as virtual tour platforms, data analytics tools, and collaborative communication platforms. These technologies not only boost the efficiency of deal-making but also give a competitive advantage in recognizing opportunities and simplifying operations.

2. Build a Strong Online Presence

Lesson Learned:

A good web presence is vital for attracting new sellers, investors, and partners. Successful virtual wholesalers recognize the value of having a reputable and engaging brand across digital channels.

Application:

Invest time in developing intriguing content, leveraging social media, and keeping a professional website. Consistent branding and communication develop confidence with stakeholders and position virtual wholesalers as competent and dependable partners in the real estate journey.

3. Leverage Data for Informed Decision-Making

Lesson Learned:

Data is a valuable tool in virtual wholesaling. Successful acquisitions are generally the product of rigorous data research, including market trends, property prices, and historical data. Data-driven decision-making eliminates risks and enhances the possibility of successful transactions.

Application:

Utilize data analytics technologies to obtain and evaluate important information. Develop predictive algorithms to anticipate property prices and find prospective possibilities. Informed judgments based on extensive data help to the success of virtual negotiations.

4. Prioritize Communication and Collaboration:

Lesson Learned:

Clear and efficient communication is crucial in virtual wholesaling. Successful sales are typically the consequence of smooth coordination among virtual teams, sellers, and investors. Virtual wholesalers that focus on communication develop solid connections that remain.

Application:

Implement collaborative communication tools and establish regular check-ins with remote team members, sellers, and investors. Clear communication fosters trust and ensures that everyone involved in the deal is aligned with expectations and goals.

5. Cultivate Adaptability and Resilience

Lesson Learned:

The real estate landscape, even in the virtual realm, is dynamic and subject to change. Successful virtual wholesalers demonstrate adaptability and resilience in the face of challenges, regulatory changes, and market fluctuations.

Application:

Develop a mindset that embraces change and uncertainty. Stay informed about industry trends, regulatory updates, and economic shifts. Being adaptable allows virtual wholesalers to pivot when necessary and navigate obstacles with resilience.

6. Invest in Continuous Learning

Lesson Learned:

The learning path never stops in virtual wholesaling. Successful professionals in this sector appreciate the necessity of remaining educated about industry developments, technology improvements, and best practices.

Application:

Allocate time and resources for continual education. Attend industry conventions, engage in webinars, and remain connected with real estate groups. Continuous learning guarantees that virtual wholesalers stay at the forefront of market developments and can react to evolving difficulties.

In the domain of virtual real estate dealings, these principles learned from successful initiatives serve as guideposts for individuals navigating the digital terrain. By embracing technology, developing a strong online presence, using data, emphasizing communication, fostering agility, and engaging in continuous learning, virtual wholesalers may pave the road to success in the dynamic and growing world of digital real estate transactions.

CONCLUSION

In the ever-evolving real estate market, the route toward virtual success is both fascinating and dynamic. As you traverse the digital environment of virtual real estate wholesaling, remember that success is not only about sales; it's about embracing innovation, fostering resilience, and employing technology to disrupt established procedures.

From the core concepts of embracing technology and developing a strong online presence to the subtle methods of data-driven decision-making and cross-border navigation, your path in virtual real estate is a tapestry of various experiences and continual learning.

As you continue on this route, bear in mind the significance of teamwork and communication.

Whether it's cultivating a collaborative virtual team or mastering the art of social media, effective engagement is vital to forging lasting connections and establishing your presence in the virtual real estate market.

The experiences of visionary leaders and tech-savvy businesses portrayed in these principles act as beacons of inspiration. Draw lessons from their experiences, but also realize that your path is uniquely yours. Adaptability and resilience will be your compass as you manage hurdles and grab opportunities.

As you think about the ideas, actions, and inspiring experiences presented, visualize your role in defining the future of virtual real estate. With each strategic decision, technical progress, and collaborative effort, you are contributing to the growth of an industry at the crossroads of tradition and innovation.

Your road to virtual real estate success is a continual narrative that you write with every transaction, every partnership, and every embrace of technology innovation. So, take the lessons learned, use them with purpose, and let your adventure in virtual real estate be a tribute to the transformational power of vision, flexibility, and tenacity.

Here's to building your route to virtual real estate success, a journey that offers not only cash but the fulfillment of your dreams in the digital frontier of real estate wholesaling.